THE CAUSE OF
MOSQUITOES'
SORROW

THE CAUSE OF
MOSQUITOES' SORROW

**Beginnings, Blunders and
Breakthroughs in Science**

SURENDRA VERMA

ICON BOOKS

Icon Books Ltd, The Old Dairy, Brook Road,
Thriplow, Cambridge SG8 7RG
email: info@iconbooks.co.uk
www.iconbooks.co.uk

Sold in the UK, Europe, South Africa and Asia
by Faber & Faber Ltd, 3 Queen Square,
London WC1N 3AU
or their agents

Distributed in the UK, Europe, South Africa and Asia
by TBS Ltd, TBS Distribution Centre, Colchester Road
Frating Green, Colchester CO7 7DW

This edition published in Australia in 2007
by Allen & Unwin Pty Ltd, PO Box 8500,
83 Alexander Street, Crows Nest, NSW 2065

Distributed in Canada by
Penguin Books Canada,
90 Eglinton Avenue East, Suite 700,
Toronto, Ontario M4P 2YE

ISBN 978-1840468-31-1

Typeset in 11pt Minion by Wayzgoose

Printed and bound in the UK
by Clays of Bungay

Contents

About the author

Surendra Verma is a science journalist based in Melbourne, Australia. He is the author of *The Mystery of the Tunguska Fireball* (Icon, 2005), *The Little Book of Scientific Principles, Theories & Things* (New Holland, 2005; Sterling Publishing, 2006) and *Why Aren't They Here?: The Question of Life on Other Worlds* (Icon, 2007).

Introduction

Graphic designers often symbolise creativity with a sparkling light bulb. This symbol has now won the approval of neuroscientists. They have found that a small region on the right side of the brain shows a striking increase in electrical activity – its functional magnetic resonance imaging (fMRI) scan literally lights up – when people experience a sudden eureka moment.

Thomas Alva Edison would have been pleased to hear this news. The technological genius, who gave us the aphorism 'Genius is one per cent inspiration and ninety-nine per cent perspiration', perspired for fourteen months while searching for the right filament for his invention. At last – after experimenting with thousands of different sorts of fibres (including the hair from the beards of some of the men in his laboratory) – he produced, in the words of the *New York Herald* of 21 December 1879, 'a light that is a little globe of sunshine, a veritable Aladdin's lamp'.

Not all scientific breakthroughs have been made with perspiration – some happened by accident, by pure luck, or simply appeared in dreams. Some 'breakthroughs' actually turned out to be awful mistakes. Many were the result of scientific ignorance at the time – while others were perhaps the deliberate deceptions of scientists desperate for recognition and glory, as hinted in this 'Researchers' prayer'.

> *Grant, oh God, Thy benedictions*
> *On my theory's predictions*
> *Lest the facts, when verified,*
> *Show Thy servant to have lied.*

> *Proceedings of the Chemical Society*, January 1963

The Cause of Mosquitoes' Sorrow traces a winding route of scientific beginnings, blunders and breakthroughs over the past four millennia, and uncovers the fascinating personalities behind them, their creative processes of discovery and their triumphs or tragedies.

The ghost of Swedish chemist Svante Arrhenius, who in 1896 first warned of global warming, will smile when that energy-saving breakthrough, the compact fluorescent bulb that uses only a quarter of the electricity, finally supersedes Edison's incandescent bulb forever. However, while human curiosity continues to thrive, the 'little globe of sunshine' will remain with us, a symbol of those memorable eureka moments that herald scientific breakthroughs.

Happy reading!

Pi-eyed after all those years

Unknown Egyptian mathematicians

Pi is a never-ending number; it takes infinite digits to express it as a decimal number.

What do supercomputers do for recreation? Some play chess; others compute the value of pi. The latest record for computing the value is to 1,241,100,000,000 decimal places. This was achieved in 2002 by a Tokyo University supercomputer. Why would you compute pi to trillions of digits when, even for designing a space probe, you don't need to know the value to more than a few digits? Like George Mallory, of Mount Everest fame, any pi fan would say: 'Because it is there.'

Pi has captured the imagination of mathematicians since ancient times. From an ancient papyrus roll written in *c.* 1700 BC by the Egyptian scribe Ahmes, we learn that Egyptian mathematicians used 3.16 as the value of pi. Archimedes' major mathematical contribution was approximating this value to 3.14 (the correct value is 3.14159 …). Even Newton was tempted. He calculated the value to fifteen decimal places but was never proud of his achievement. 'I am ashamed to tell you to how many figures I have carried out these computations, having no other business at the time', he wrote to a friend.

If you have no other business at the moment and are tempted to memorise the value of pi to twenty decimal places, here's a mnemonic (just count the number of letters in each word to give you the value of each decimal place).

> *Sir, I bear a rhyme excelling*
> *In mystic force and magic spelling*
> *Celestial sprites elucidate*
> *All my own striving can't relate.*

'All things are water'

Thales (*c.* 624–*c.* 545 BC)

Thales was the first to ask what the universe was made of.

Thales, the founder of Greek science, mathematics and philosophy, answered the question by saying that 'all things are water' and anything that did not appear to be water had once been water and had been modified by some natural process. 'Water is the first principle, or the element, of nature,' he said. This view may not seem scientific to us, but against the background of mythology from which it arose, it was revolutionary. He offered rational rather than supernatural explanation. His theory was derived from observed facts.

Thales also made the first accurate prediction of a solar eclipse. It's not known how he arrived at the date of the eclipse – 28 May 585 BC – but his interest in stars is supported by this famous story. One night he was gazing at the sky as he walked and fell into a ditch. A girl lifted him out and remarked sarcastically: 'Here's a man who wants to study stars, but cannot see what lies at his feet.'

In *c.* 350 BC the Greek philosopher Aristotle proposed that the world was made from four elements: earth, water, air and fire. Each of these elements was characterised by two of the four opposite qualities: hot, cold, wet and dry. Earth was cold and dry, air hot and wet, water cold and wet, and fire hot and dry. Aristotle's influence was extraordinary and his view dominated scientific thinking until it was displaced in AD 1661 by the idea of chemical elements (see p. 34).

A strange idea!

Pythagoras (*c.* 580–500 BC)

c. **530** BC
Greece

Pythagoras was the first ancient Greek philosopher to propose that Earth was spherical.

'Earth is a sphere floating in space', he declared. A grave silence fell upon the lecture room, which was crowded with enthusiastic hearers of all ranks. They were amazed to hear this. They wondered how they could live on a sphere! 'It's not a flat disc floating on the air as believed by other philosophers. The circle is the most perfect geometrical form; the sphere is the most perfect of all solid figures. Hence Earth, the Sun, the stars, the planets and the universe as a whole, must be spherical', the speaker, known as Pythagoras of Samos, argued.

Pythagoras travelled widely and attained the highest eminence in mathematics. While travelling in Egypt, he discovered his famous theorem: in a right-angled triangle, the square on the hypotenuse is the sum of the squares on the other two sides. After travelling for more than 30 years he settled in Croton, a Greek colony in southern Italy, where he founded a philosophical and religious school. His lectures were so inspiring that some of his pupils formed themselves into a brotherhood for continuing his ideas. They called themselves Pythagoreans.

Pythagoras's 'strange' idea of the round Earth was based on his observation that Earth casts a circular shadow on the Moon during eclipses. It was accepted by Aristotle and other Greek philosophers and became common knowledge. Pythagoras is also supposed to have coined the Geek word *philosophos* ('lover of wisdom', philosopher).

Democritus's opinion

Democritus (c. 460–c. 370 BC)

'The universe is composed of atoms and empty space, everything else is merely thought to exist', said Democritus.

The notion of the atom may have originated in Babylon, Egypt or India, but the first concept remarkably similar to that of modern science was proposed by the 5th-century Greek philosopher Leucippus. He said that everything was composed of tiny particles so small that nothing smaller was conceivable. Democritus, a pupil of Leucippus, adopted and extended his teacher's ideas. Democritus taught that matter was composed of empty space and an infinite number of tiny particles that were indivisible. He called them *atomos*, or atoms (*atomos*, in fact, means 'indivisible'). He believed that they were always in motion and as they moved about they collided; sometimes they interlocked and held together, sometimes they rebounded from a collision.

When he became blind towards the end of his life, Democritus maintained that what he could see with the 'soul's eye' was truer and more beautiful than things seen with the bodily eyes. He decided to starve himself to death. When he found that he was likely to die during a festival, which would then deprive his sister of the festivities, he prolonged his life by inhaling the aroma of hot loaves of bread.

Aristotle and other Greek philosophers rejected Democritus's opinion. They preferred to believe in their four 'elements' – earth, air, fire and water – out of which the whole world was created, and Democritus's atomic theory was lost for 2,000 years.

It's true because Aristotle said so

Aristotle (384–322 BC)

Aristotle founded the science of zoology.

Aristotle's most successful scientific writings were in biology. He was a meticulous observer and studied first-hand more than 500 species of animals, dissecting nearly 50 of them. He discussed human and animal anatomy and the function of the body's organs (though he erroneously suggested the heart to be the site of consciousness, not the brain); described how chicks developed inside eggs, and baby mammals inside their mothers; distinguished whales and dolphins from fish; studied the social organisation of bees and said that there was only one ruler in the hive (though he called it the 'king' not the 'queen'); correctly recognised that dolphins were air-breathing animals and not fish, as people believed; and attempted to classify animals according to features they had in common – his books on animals are filled with hundreds of these observations, some of which weren't confirmed until many centuries later.

Aristotle's work on animals was the greatest such collection of the time, but it wasn't free of errors. The greatest compliment to Aristotle's talents as a biologist comes from Darwin, who said that the modern biologists Linnaeus and Cuvier were 'mere schoolboys to Aristotle'.

Aristotle is still admired as a great philosopher, but in matters of science he was wrong a lot of the time. Yet for more than 2,000 years his ideas ruled scientific thinking and were accepted without question. There has never been a scientist whose teachings received a kind of divine reverence for so long.

The Botanical Man

Theophrastus (*c.* 372–*c.* 287 BC)

Theophrastus began the science of botany.

Theophrastus was a student of Aristotle and succeeded him as the head of Lyceum, the academy founded by Aristotle. He was the first to ask questions such as 'What are the similarities and differences between plants?' and seek scientific answers to them. He divided the plant world into two kingdoms, the flowering and the flowerless, and classified more than 500 species of plants into one of four groups: trees, shrubs, under shrubs and herbs. He also coined new terms to describe their structures and functions.

His botanical works show his crisp and concise observations, proving that he was an acute observer of the life histories of plants. In ancient Greece the olive tree was the symbol of winning and of compromising (an olive branch is still the symbol of peace); and victors at the games in Olympia were awarded crowns made of olive branches. Theophrastus described plants used in Olympia more than four centuries before his time and mentioned 'the wild olive at Olympia, from which the wreaths for the games are made'.

Described by the 18th-century Swiss biologist Albrecht von Haller as the 'first true botanist', Theophrastus influenced botanists for centuries to come. He's remembered now not so much for his botanical works, as for satirical character sketches of various types of individuals – such as the Officious Man ('promises things beyond power'), the Boastful Man ('boasts how he served with Alexander') and the Man of Petty Ambition ('anxious to sit next to the patron') – which can still be recognised today.

Step-by-step road to learning

c. **300** BC
Alexandria

Euclid (flourished *c.* 300 BC)

An algorithm is a set of rules to solve a specific problem.

Euclid's name is inextricably linked with geometry, for he wrote the most famous geometry book of all time. *Elements* was the only textbook of geometry for 2,000 years and its basic rules are still taught in schools. Euclid is also known for admonishing King Ptolemy I of Egypt when he asked if there was an easier way to learn geometry, by replying: 'There is no royal road to geometry.' His appearance in this book is for being the writer of one of the oldest algorithms known: an algorithm for calculating the greatest common divisor of two whole numbers.

However, the word algorithm is relatively recent. It comes from the name of the 9th-century Arabian mathematician Muhammad ibn Musa al-Khwarizmi. His last name – Mūsā al-Khwārizmī – was Latinised as *algorismus* and used to refer to the art of calculating. It became algorithm in English.

In 1937 Alan Turing, the brilliant British mathematician famous for breaking the German navy's Enigma code during the Second World War, gave algorithm a mathematically precise definition. He did it by developing a theoretical computer. The imaginary machine – with two or more possible states, which reacted to an input to produce an output – obeyed instructions set out in an algorithm. The method of applying an algorithm to an input to obtain an output is called a computation. The Turing machine provided the theoretical basis for the development of digital computers. Ada Lovelace wrote the first algorithm for a computer in 1843 (see p. 67).

Another strange idea!

Aristarchus of Samos (c. 310–230 BC)

Aristarchus was the first Greek philosopher to propose that Earth moved around the Sun.

In the 3rd century BC people believed that Earth was the centre of the universe, and the Sun moved around it. In his book *Sand Reckoner*, Archimedes, a younger contemporary of Aristarchus, credits him with holding the hypothesis that Earth was not at the centre of the universe, but that it moved around the Sun. This idea of a moving Earth seemed utterly strange in those ancient days and it was, of course, rejected by his contemporaries. They thought it ridiculous to imagine that anything as big and solid as Earth could be in motion!

Aristarchus was the first astronomer to apply mathematics to astronomical observations in order to make logical deductions. His only surviving book, *On Sizes and Distances of the Sun and the Moon*, deals with relative measurements of the Sun, the Moon and Earth. From his calculations, he deduced that the distance between the Sun and the Moon was nineteen to twenty times that between the Moon and Earth. The true figure is about 390 times. From a lunar eclipse he estimated that Earth must have twice the diameter of the Moon, although the true figure is about double this. Although his calculations were wrong, his mathematical measuring techniques were strictly scientific.

Aristarchus's hypothesis of the Sun-centred universe was revived in 1543 by Copernicus (see p. 24). That's why Aristarchus is sometimes called the Copernicus of Antiquity.

The first 'Eureka!'

Archimedes (*c.* 287–212 BC)

A body immersed in a fluid is subject to an upward force equal in magnitude to the weight of fluid it displaces.

Today Archimedes, the greatest scientist, mathematician and mechanical genius of antiquity, is mostly remembered for the tale of his running naked through the streets shouting: 'Eureka! Eureka!' King Hiero of Syracuse, suspecting that his goldsmith had adulterated his newly built gold crown with silver, asked Archimedes to find out the truth without damaging the crown. Archimedes discovered that the crown was adulterated along with his famous scientific principle at bath time. He noticed that – when getting into a tub full of water – the level of water rose as he got in. Archimedes' legendary bath gave all scientists a word with which to hail their discoveries and an excuse, if they wish, to run naked through the streets.

Less well known is the story of Archimedes' tragic death. When the Roman general Marcellus captured Syracuse, a Greek city in Sicily, he gave orders that Archimedes was to be left unharmed. But the orders never reached the detachment of Roman soldiers who found him engaged in his backyard drawing some complicated geometrical figures on sand. Seeing the soldiers, Archimedes shouted: 'Do not touch my drawings!' One of the soldiers drove a spear through the body of the great thinker, when he could well have been contemplating something further for the benefit of humankind.

The Romans buried him with honours and marked his tomb by a sphere inscribed in a cylinder. He had asked that at his death his grave should be marked with this particular drawing, with an inscription giving the difference between volumes within and outside the sphere.

See also THE PRINCIPLE OF THE LEVER, p. 12.

'Give me a place to stand and I'll move Earth'

Archimedes (c. 287–212 BC)

The lever (used with an appropriate fulcrum or pivot) magnifies force and speed.

Archimedes arrived at the principle by reasoning that two equal weights suspended at the ends of a uniform rod, which is suspended at its centre, will balance each other. Legend has it that when he discovered the lever's incredible ability to make heavy lifting easier he was so excited by the discovery he boasted to King Hiero of Syracuse, his kinsman and friend.

'King Hiero begged Archimedes to put his proposition into execution, and show him some great weight moved by a slight force', writes the Greek historian Plutarch in his book, *Life of Marcellus* (AD 75). 'Archimedes, therefore, fixed upon a three-master merchantman of the royal fleet, which had been dragged ashore by the great labours of many men, and after putting on board many passengers and customary freight, he seated himself at a distance from her, and without great effort, but quietly setting in motion with his hand a system of compound pulleys, drew her towards him smoothly and evenly, as though she were gliding through the water.' The crowd was spellbound to see a mortal single-handedly lift a fully loaded ship.

The lever is one of the six types of simple machines – lever; wheel and axle; pulley (the lever family); ramp; wedge; and screw (the inclined plane family) – which all form part of complex machines. A playground seesaw is the common example of the lever in action.

See also BUOYANCY, p. 11.

An astonishing achievement

c. **240** BC
Alexandria

Eratosthenes (c. 275–194 BC)

Eratosthenes used simple geometry to make a remarkably accurate measurement of Earth.

It was the mid-day of summer solstice. Eratosthenes was walking in the marketplace in Alexandria, a Greek colony in Egypt, when he overheard someone say: 'At this time there is no shadow anywhere in my hometown Syene. If you look into a deep well at noon, the Sun reflects directly from the water in the bottom of the well.' Eratosthenes stuck a tall pole into the ground in a perpendicular position and measured that the pole cast a shadow whose length was one-fiftieth of the height of the pole. With the aid of his geometrical instruments he found that the Sun's rays were falling at an angle of 7.2°, which is one-fiftieth of 360°.

He reasoned that the surface of Earth was curved, resulting in the angle of the Sun's rays being different in different locations. As the Sun's rays are parallel, he knew from geometry that the size of the measured angle equalled the size of the angle between the two lines drawn from Earth's centre to Syene (now Aswan) and Alexandria respectively. Knowing the distance between the two places, he calculated that the circumference of Earth was 50 times that distance. Eratosthenes' value comes to 39,350 kilometres, as against a true average length of 40,033 kilometres.

We remember Eratosthenes not only for measuring the size of Earth, but also for the 'Sieve of Eratosthenes', a method for identifying prime numbers. He became blind in 195 BC and died the following year of voluntary starvation.

c. **200** BC
India

Is it something, is it nothing?

Unknown Hindu mathematicians

There are two uses of zero: as a number itself meaning 'nothing', and as an empty place indicator in our place-value number system.

The zero, as we know it to be today, first appeared in AD 458 in a Hindu cosmology text, but indirect evidence shows that it may have been in use as early as 200 BC. At first, it was denoted by a dot, which was replaced later by the familiar circular symbol, 0. The oldest zero in history appeared in Babylonia in the 4th century BC. The Babylonian zero, used to mark an absent unit in their sexagesimal (base-60) counting system, did not signify 'the number 0', and did not have the meaning of 'nothing' as in '5 – 5 = 0'.

In the 8th century AD the Indian place-value system of numerals based on 1, 2, 3, 4, 5, 6, 7, 8, 9 and 0 – now known as the decimal or base-10 number system – spread to Arabic countries. In the 12th century, Italian mathematician Leonardo Fibonacci introduced the concept of zero to Europe. The name 'zero' comes from the Arabic *ṣifr* which also gives us the word 'cipher'. Ancient Hindu mathematicians called it *sunya*, meaning empty.

You will never say zero is nothing, if you can answer any of the following questions.

$n \div 0 = ?$ (any number divided by zero)
$n^0 = ?$ (any number raised to the power of zero)
$0^0 = ?$ (zero raised to the power of zero).

Just couldn't keep away

Pliny the Elder (23–79)

AD **77**
Rome

Historia Naturalis **was the first encyclopedia of science.**

The Roman statesman and scholar Pliny the Elder, or Gaius Plinius Secundus, wrote about 75 books on history, grammar, rhetoric and natural history. His only surviving book *Historia Naturalis* is the most comprehensive survey of scientific learning in the ancient world. In 37 volumes of natural history it covers cosmology, astronomy, meteorology, geography, zoology, botany, agriculture, medicine, minerals and metals.

Pliny describes the subject of his book as 'the world of nature or, in other words, life'; and admits that it contains little original work and is a compilation of facts from 4,000 other authors. Written in Latin, *Historia* was frequently copied throughout the centuries. It was first printed in 1469 in Venice, and translated into English in 1601.

When Mount Vesuvius blew its top in 79 and buried the cities of Pompeii and Herculaneum, Pliny was in command of a Roman fleet stationed in the Bay of Naples. His nephew, now known as Pliny the Younger, recorded the last day of an extraordinary scholar who died in the act of collecting facts. Pliny the Elder just couldn't keep away from the erupting volcano, such was its scientific interest to him. He ordered a boat to hug the shore so he could observe the volcano closely. 'The flames and smell of sulphur, which always tells you the flames are coming, made the others run away', writes Pliny the Younger. 'When daylight returned on the 26th – two days after the last day he had [been] seen – his body was found intact and uninjured, still fully clothed and looking more like sleep than death.'

'The ambrosial food of gods'

Ptolemy (*c.* 100–*c.* 170)

Almagest **was the first complete treatise of mathematical astronomy.**

The Great Library of Alexandria was the cultural centre of Ptolemy's time. The library had amassed more than 400,000 scrolls since it was established in the 3rd century BC. Ptolemy studied the works of the astronomers and mathematicians of the antiquity at the library, and built out of them a new system of the cosmos. He described this system in a Greek book, which was dubbed 'the great treatise' by his admirers. In the 9th century it was translated into the Arabic under the title *Almagest* ('the greatest' in Arabic). It outlines a theory of the universe – with Earth immovable and at the centre of the universe – known as the Ptolemaic system. This system dominated astronomical thinking for fourteen centuries until it was demolished by Copernicus in 1543.

Almagest deals with the planetary motions in a unique way: planets revolving in a circle round a moving centre. These cycles and epicycles puzzled the astronomers for centuries. 'If the Lord Almighty had consulted me before embarking upon creation, I should have recommended something simpler', sighed Alfonso the Wise, a 13th-century Spanish king, when he first studied the Ptolemaic system.

But Ptolemy was no ordinary astronomer. He asserted: 'I know that I am mortal, and ephemeral; but when I scan the multitudinous circling spirals of the stars, no longer do I touch the earth with my feet, but sit with Zeus himself, and take my fill of the ambrosial food of gods.'

The riddle of Diophantus

Diophantus (flourished *c.* 250)

Diophantus is considered the founder of algebra.

Almost nothing is known about Diophantus's life. The only details we have come from a riddle about him in the Greek anthology compiled by Metrodorus around AD 500.

> Diophantus's boyhood lasted $\frac{1}{6}$ of his life. He grew a beard after $\frac{1}{12}$ more. After a $\frac{1}{7}$ more of his life he married. Five years later he had a son. The son lived $\frac{1}{2}$ as long as his father and the father died 4 years after his son.

If x is the age of Diophantus, the riddle gives the equation:

$$x = \tfrac{1}{6}x + \tfrac{1}{12}x + \tfrac{1}{7}x + 5 + \tfrac{1}{2}x + 4$$

which when solved gives $x = 84$ as the age of Diophantus.

Diophantus is best known for his *Arithmetica*, a work on the solution of algebraic equations. *Arithmetica* is one of the most influential books in the history of mathematics. Diophantus did not introduce today's algebraic notation, but he was the first to use symbols for unknown quantities.

The symbols that are used today were introduced by Descartes (see p. 31). He decided that the letters at the beginning of the alphabet, *a*, *b* and *c*, would be used for known numbers and those at the end of the alphabet, *x*, *y* and *z*, for the unknowns. The word 'algebra' comes from the Arabic word *al-jabr*, meaning 'the reunion of broken parts'. This word appears in the title of a book on algebra, *Kitab al-jabr w'al-muqabala*, written by al-Khwārizmī (see p. 9) in *c.* 825.

The 'mad' master of optics

1038
Egypt

Alhazen (965–1040)

Alhazen's work on optics marked the beginning of the science of optics and influenced scientists for centuries.

Abu Ali al-Hassan Ibn al-Haytham (known to the Western world as Alhazen) was born in Basra, Iraq. According to a popular story, al-Hakim, the Caliph of Egypt, invited him to Egypt to regulate the flooding of the Nile. When Alhazen realised that this was no mean feat, he pretended to be mad to escape from the wrath of the cruel and eccentric al-Hakim (known as the Mad Caliph, he once ordered the killing of all dogs because their barking annoyed him). After al-Hakim's death in 1021 Alhazen lived a normal life in a house near Azhar Mosque in Cairo, writing, experimenting and teaching.

In his greatest scientific work *Kitab-al-Manazir* (*The Book of Optics*), Alhazen rejected the theory of the ancient Greeks that vision is the result of the eye giving out rays of light and reaching the object. Instead, he proposed, correctly, that vision was made possible by rays of light reflecting from an object into the eye. He also explained how lenses work and attributed their magnifying power to the curvature of their surfaces.

Alhazen, who is now recognised as one of the most eminent Islamic scientists of the Middle Ages, was also the first to describe the camera obscura (the first drawings appear in Leonardo da Vinci's 1490 notebooks). It consisted of a darkened room (camera means room in Latin) with a small round hole through which light passed to form an image on the wall opposite the opening.

Breaking the law

Bhaskara II (1114–85)

c. **1150**
India

Bhaskara was the first to propose a perpetual motion machine, a machine that would run forever without consuming energy.

Bhaskara (also known as Bhaskaracharya, 'Bhaskara the Learned') has a respected place in the history of mathematics. He wrote the first works using the decimal number system. He also has a special place in the annals of perpetual motion machines as the designer of a wheel that could turn forever, although he never built it. The wheel, with containers of mercury around its rim, was designed to rotate constantly, because the wheel would always be heavier on one side of the axle.

This idea, like the ideas of zero and decimal numbers, re-appeared in Arabic writings. From the Islamic world it reached the Western world. Over the centuries numerous scientists and engineers tried – and failed miserably – to build perpetual motion machines. However, failure did not stop them patenting their creations. The first patent for a perpetual motion machine was granted in 1635 in England. Most patent offices now refuse to grant patents for perpetual motion machines without working models.

Perpetual motion violates the laws of thermodynamics. It defies the sacrosanct law of conservation of energy (the first law of thermo-dynamics, see p. 69), that no machine can produce more energy than it uses. The second law of thermodynamics (see p. 78) places constraints on machines, such as car engines, that do useful work by tapping heat energy from burning fuel. This law demands that heat must flow from a hotter to a colder body. This means the machine must lose some energy when heat is converted into useful work.

The oldest keyboard

Unknown Chinese mathematicians

1377
China

The abacus was the first important calculating device invented.

The abacus (*suanpan* in Chinese) as we know it today is simply a rectangular frame of rods with beads strung on them. A typical Chinese abacus has thirteen columns, each one divided into an upper deck and a lower deck. The lower deck has five beads in each column; the lower deck, two beads per column. The beads in the upper deck are worth five times the beads in the lower deck. The first column represents single units, the second tens, the third hundreds, and so on. This means you can do calculations with numbers up to 10 trillion. If you are an expert, you can carry out not only addition, subtraction, multiplication and division problems, but can also work out fractions, and square and cube roots.

We do not know for sure when the first abacus came into use. Some form of abacus was used as long ago as 3000 BC in the Middle East. However, the abacus we're familiar with came from China. Historians dispute the exact date, but the earliest known illustration of an abacus appears in a 1377 book printed from wood engravings, and the device became popular from the second half of the 16th century. In 1822 the French mathematician Jean-Victor Poncelet, the founder of modern projective geometry, introduced the abacus into Europe.

In this age of calculators and computers why bother with a wooden frame? There's a very good reason: if you know how to use the world's oldest keyboard, it's as fast as the electronic calculator on addition and subtraction problems.

'Very clear and proper lettering'

Johannes Gutenberg (c. 1395–1468)

The printing press was one of the most important technical breakthroughs in history.

Movable type was invented in China (made from clay in c. 1041; made from hardwood in c. 1297). But in Europe in the early 14th century there were only handwritten books or some short texts, printed using wooden blocks into which words had been carved.

Gutenberg was a young engraver and gem-cutter when he thought of using movable type to compose whole books. He experimented over several years, borrowing large sums of money to cover costs. He made moulds of letters for casting individual characters in metal. He invented devices for composing the types on a wooden plate and for inking the composition evenly, and finally a hand-printing press for making impressions of the plates on paper.

He tested his press by printing an old German poem over and over again. He was now ready for the job he'd been dreaming of for years: printing the whole Bible in Latin. He composed 1,283 pages of 42 lines each, and printed 180 copies. The first book ever printed from movable type was ready in 1455. Proof that the first printed book was indeed a bestseller is found in a letter dated 12 March 1455, where the writer enthused: 'I did not see any complete Bibles, but I did see a certain number of five-page booklets of several of the books of the Bible, with very clear and proper lettering, and without any faults … even before the books were finished, there were customers ready to buy them.'

Medical revolution of the Renaissance

1530s
Switzerland

Paracelsus (1493–1541)

The true purpose of alchemy is not to make gold but to prepare medicine, declared Paracelsus.

Dr Theophrastus von Hohenheim was so much impressed with the works of Celsus, a 1st-century Roman medical encyclopedist, that he took the name Paracelsus, meaning 'beyond Celsus'. In Paracelsus's time, the practice of medicine was based on the ideas of the ancient Greek physicians Hippocrates and Galen. Basically, sickness was the sign of imbalance of the four humours (bodily fluids) – phlegm, blood, bile and black bile – and the task of the physician was to restore balance in the body.

Paracelsus rejected these ideas and said that disease originates from external rather than internal causes. He applied his knowledge of alchemy to search for new medicines. He stressed the importance of minerals in medicine, and was the first to use the processes of alchemy – the extraction of pure metals from ores – to make medicines from compounds of antimony, arsenic, mercury and zinc (he introduced zinc to the Western world). He knew some of the compounds were poisonous, but his defence would please modern practitioners: 'It is only the dose that makes a thing a poison.'

Although his life was marked by arrogance (he called himself the 'monarch of medicine'), drunkenness and quarrelsomeness (he died after being stabbed in a tavern fight), Paracelsus revolutionised medicine by establishing the importance of chemistry in medicine. 'In experiments theories or arguments do not count', he exhorted his fellow physicians. 'We pray you not to oppose the importance of the method of experiment but to follow it without prejudice.'

The missing rib

Andreas Vesalius (1514–64)

1543
Italy

Vesalius's detailed account of human anatomy laid the foundations of modern anatomy.

In the 16th century many of the false ideas of Galen, an ancient Greek anatomist, still dominated medicine. Galen's knowledge of human anatomy was based on the dissection of apes, dogs and pigs. If Galen, for instance, said that the human heart had only two chambers (it has four), then two chambers was all it had.

Vesalius, a Belgian doctor's son, studied medicine at the University of Padua in Italy. He became particularly well versed in Galen's work, but wasn't impressed by his ideas on human anatomy. When he became a professor at the university he performed his own dissections on cadavers, inventing instruments and improvising procedures as needed. He discovered some 200 anatomical errors that Galen had made. However, it wasn't easy to displace Galen. Vesalius was ridiculed when he said that men and women have an equal number of ribs. At that time people believed that men have one rib fewer than women, because of the biblical story that Eve was created out of Adam's rib.

In 1543 Vesalius published his findings in a magnificently illustrated book *De Humani Corporis Fabrica* ('On the Fabric of the Human Body'). This anatomically accurate medical textbook continues to influence the way we look at the human body today.

1543
Poland

Sun, stand thou still

Nicolaus Copernicus (1473–1543)

De Revolutionibus Orbium Coelestium ('On the Revolutions of the Celestial Spheres') founded modern astronomy.

In this book, Copernicus rejected the ancient and commonly held wisdom that Earth stood still at the centre of the universe and that the Sun revolved around it. To the contrary, he declared that the Sun is at the centre of the solar system, with Earth and other planets revolving around it. He gave detailed accounts of the motions of Earth, the Moon and planets, and said that Earth also revolves on its axis, which accounts for why we have days and nights.

Copernicus completed the book in about 1530, but decided not to publish it. He knew that the book would be seized and destroyed by the Catholic Church as it contravened its teachings. His pupil and friend Georg Rheticus took the manuscript to Nuremberg and printed about 600 copies. A copy was sent to the author, but it arrived only a few hours before his death.

The Church duly banned the book and placed it on its index of prohibited books. However, as this verse (*c.* 1712) by the English poet Richard Blackmore testifies, Copernicus's ideas became popular long before the Church's ban ended in 1835.

> *Copernicus, who rightly did condemn*
> *This eldest system, form'd a wiser scheme;*
> *In which he leaves the sun at rest, and rolls*
> *The orb terrestrial on its proper poles;*
> *Which makes the night and day by this career,*
> *And by its flow and crooked course the year.*

A myth exploded

Tycho Brahe (1546–1601)

1572

Denmark

Brahe's observation of a supernova disproved the ancient notion that the heavens were fixed and unchanging.

In the history of astronomy, 11 November 1572 is a red-letter day, for on this date a young astronomer saw a new star blazing out in the constellation of Cassiopeia. He watched the star – as bright as Jupiter – carefully night after night until it gradually faded. He called it *nova* and in 1573 published a small book *De Nova Stella* ('A New Star') in which he suggested that stars could have a beginning, middle and end. This revolutionary idea smashed the belief of the ancient Greek astronomers that stars were fixed and unchanging. For them, anything in the sky that didn't have a regular and predictable path – this included a meteor or comet – was related to meteorological phenomena such as lightning and rainbows.

Today scientists know that Tycho (he is usually known by his first name) observed a supernova that was visible in the northern skies for nearly two years. A supernova is an old star that suddenly explodes as it blasts itself apart. The remaining matter forms a neutron star.

Tycho was an extraordinary observer of the sky. Kepler was an assistant to Tycho and after his death inherited his vast accumulation of planetary observations. Without this data, Kepler wouldn't have arrived at his own laws (see p. 28). Tycho, however, dissented from the Copernican theory and accepted without question the dogma that Earth stood still at the centre of the universe and the Sun went around it (all other planets being in orbit about the Sun and so carried around with it). 'The Sun', he declared, 'is the Leader and the King who regulates the whole harmony of planetary dance'.

The swinging chandelier

1581
Italy

Galileo Galilei (1564–1642)

A pendulum will swing at a constant time, which means it can be used for timekeeping.

Galileo was a seventeen-year-old medical student at the University of Pisa when he made this startling discovery. During Mass at the Cathedral of Pisa, he became bored and dreamily fixed his eyes on a chandelier swinging from a long rope. It seemed to him that the time of the swing was the same whether the swing was a large or small one. He used his own pulse beat – as a medical student he knew that under normal conditions our pulse beats regularly – to test his intuition. Later on he experimented with a metal ball suspended by a string – what's now know as a simple pendulum – and found that he was correct. Every swing of the ball, large or small, took the same time. This is called isochronism of the pendulum.

In 1602 he used the principle of pendulum to invent an instrument to measure the pulse rates of patients. The simple device, the pulsilogium, proved of great value to physicians. Years later, in 1641, at the age of 77 when he was totally blind, the idea of making a clock regulated by a pendulum occurred to him. His son, Vincenzio, a clever mechanic, made several drawings and models. However, the first working pendulum clock was made by the Dutch scientist Christiaan Huygens in 1656.

Galileo's discovery of the principle of pendulum paved the way for the accurate measurement of small intervals of time.

See also DIALOGUE CONCERNING THE TWO CHIEF WORLD SYSTEMS, p. 30.

No, it won't muddle the minds of students

1600
England

William Gilbert (1544–1603)

De Magnete **was the first-ever learned work on experimental physics.**

Gilbert, a distinguished physician, was the first to realise that Earth is itself a giant magnet. A compass needle would dip down at different angles at different points of the globe, but would point straight down at the North Pole (previously it was thought the compass pointed to a magnetic island somewhere in the Arctic region). He introduced an instrument called the inclinometer which navigators could use for determining latitudes during overcast days. He also distinguished between magnetism and static electricity, which were considered similar phenomena. Amber produces static electricity when rubbed with a cloth. The Greek name for amber is *elektron*, from which Gilbert coined the Latin word *electricitas* for this property that amber displayed. The word was soon anglicised to 'electricity'.

He was an astute experimenter and maintained that 'stronger reasons are obtained from sure experiments and demonstrated arguments'. He was scornful of bookish knowledge and dedicated his 'foundations of magnetic science' to those 'who look for knowledge not in books but in things themselves'.

While Gilbert was enthusiastic in support of the Copernican system, the great experimenter was incorrect when he speculated that magnetism was the actual cause of Earth's rotation. But his science was on the ball when he criticised – with the full force of invectives – claims for magnetic perpetual motion machines, exclaiming: 'May the gods damn all such sham, pilfered, distorted works, which do but muddle the minds of students.'

'The die is cast'

1619
Germany

Johannes Kepler (1571–1630)

Kepler's three laws of planetary motion are considered a major landmark in science.

'Nothing holds me; I will indulge in my sacred fury ... If you forgive me, I rejoice; if you are angry, I can bear it; the die is cast; the book is written; to be read either now or by posterity, I care not which; it may as well wait for a century for a reader.' Kepler was wild with joy and mad with the excitement when he discovered his third law of planetary motion in 1619: that the squares of the orbital periods of the planets are proportional to the cubes of their mean distances from the Sun. He had discovered his first two laws (that planets move in elliptical orbits with the Sun at one focus; and that the straight line joining the Sun and any planet sweeps out equal areas in equal periods of time) ten years earlier.

Kepler was an ardent Copernican ('The Sun not only stands in the centre of the universe, but is its moving spirit', he asserted) and his laws provided a mathematical framework for the Copernican system. The third law also helped Newton to develop his law of gravitation.

A few months before his death, Kepler wrote this epitaph for himself.

> *I used to measure the heavens,*
> *Now I measure the shadows of the earth.*
> *Although my mind was heaven-bound,*
> *The shadow of my body lies here.*

Unfortunately, a few years after his death, his burial site was permanently destroyed in the Thirty Years War (1618–48).

'My trust is in my love of truth'

1628
England

William Harvey (1578–1657)

The blood, pushed by the heart, moves 'as it were, in a circle'.

Since blood is bright red in the arteries and bluish in the veins, physicians in Harvey's time believed that there were two distinct systems of blood flow in the body. They also believed that blood was made in the liver and flowed through the septum (the dividing wall) of the heart before being absorbed by the body.

For years Harvey dissected many animals to observe the functioning of the heart. From these experiments he concluded that the heart is a pump made of muscle. It has four chambers: two upper auricles and two lower ventricles. The blood is pumped by the left ventricle through the arteries, and it returns through the veins to the right auricle. It then passes through the right ventricle which pumps it to the lungs, where it changes from a bluish to a bright red colour. It returns from the lung to the left auricle, then passes through the left ventricle. Thus it circulates continuously.

Harvey waited for years before publishing his findings in 1628; he was afraid that they wouldn't be accepted as 'respect for antiquity influences all men: still the die is cast and my trust is in my love of truth'. He was ridiculed as a *'circulator'* (the Latin slang for 'quack'). 'All the physicians were against his opinion, and envied him; many wrote against him', notes John Aubrey, in his gossipy *Brief Lives* (*c.* 1680). 'But in about 20 or 30 years of time, it was received in all the universities of the world.'

1632
Italy

A trial and a public abjuration

Galileo Galilei (1564–1642)

Dialogue **marked the transition from the dark days of the Middle Ages to the modern era of science.**

He knelt before the awful tribunal of the Inquisition to make a recantation of his belief in the Copernican system. 'I, Galileo Galilei, son of the late Vincenzio Galilei of Florence, aged 70 years, being brought personally to judgment ... abandon the false opinion that the Sun is the centre of the world and immovable and that Earth is not the centre of the world and moves and that I must not hold, defend or teach the said false doctrine in any manner ...' With this public abjuration ended the most tragic trial in the history of science.

When he published his *Dialogue*, which was an explanation and extension of the Copernican system, Galileo was tried in 1633 for heresy before the Roman Inquisition, found guilty and sentenced to indefinite house confinement. Under the threat of torture he agreed to 'confess'.

In Galileo's book the dialogue is between Salviati, a philosopher who represents the views of Galileo; Simplicio, a philosopher who is a follower of Aristotle; and Sagredo, an intelligent layman. When Simplicio asks: 'How do you deduce that it is not Earth, but the Sun, which is at the centre of the revolutions of planets?', Salviati replies: 'This is deducted from the most obvious and therefore most powerfully convincing observations.' Galileo was the first to study the heavens through the telescope. His evidence for the Copernican theory of the solar system was based on these convincing observations.

See also PENDULUM, p. 26.

The union of algebra and geometry

1637
France

René Descartes (1596–1650)

In analytical geometry (also known as coordinate or Cartesian geometry), methods of algebra are used to solve the problems of geometry.

Equations and formulae are easier to explore than the cobweb of points, curves and lines. The basic feature of analytical geometry is that a point in space can be completely fixed if we know its distances from three arbitrarily chosen lines of references that are at right angles to each other. These distances, usually labelled x, y and z, are called the coordinates of the point, and the lines of reference are normally referred to as x-, y- and z-axes. The concept of longitude and latitude is also based on analytical geometry.

In his early years Descartes, a philosopher and mathematician, was sceptical of almost everything, even his own existence. He lost this scepticism after reaching the conclusion: *'Cogito ergo sum'* ('I think, therefore I am') – arguably the single best-known philosophical statement. There's a story that he came up with the idea of analytical geometry when he watched a fly crawling on the ceiling of his room, and realised its position could be defined by its distances from the two adjacent walls. And, as he liked lying in bed late every morning and meditating, perhaps this story is true. Analytical geometry appears as an appendix, *La géométrie*, in his 1637 masterpiece, *Discours de la method* ('A Discourse on the Method').

'Descartes did not revise geometry, he created it', declares E. T. Bell in his authoritative biographical volume, *Men of Mathematics* (1937).

Algebraic melodrama

Pierre de Fermat (1601–65)

Fermat's tricky problem tantalised even the greatest of mathematicians for 356 years until it was finally solved in 1993. It continues to inspire poets and songwriters.

> *I knew, I swore*
> *That elegant symmetry*
> *Of x squared plus y squared*
> *Is square of z*
> *Could not be repeated if n were three or more!*

Sings a character in *Fermat's Last Tango* (2000), a musical by Joshua Rosenblum and Joanne Sidney Lessner, which captures the drama and passion associated with the centuries-long quest to solve Fermat's infuriating theorem.

Fermat, an amateur mathematician, had been reading Diophantus's *Arithmetica* (see p. 17) when he came across a problem asking the solution of the equation $x^2 + y^2 = z^2$. He wrote in the margin of the book: 'There are no whole-number solutions of the equation $x^n + y^n = z^n$ for n greater than 2. I have discovered a truly marvellous proof of this theorem, which this margin is too narrow to contain.' This is Fermat's famous last theorem.

After seven years' dedicated work, British-born Andrew Wiles, a professor of mathematics at Princeton University, finally solved the problem in 1993. Extols an unknown poet:

> *While the ghost*
> *Of Fermat smiles*
> *Give three cheers*
> *For Andrew Wiles.*

Nature does not abhor a vacuum

1643
Italy

Evangelista Torricelli (1608–47)

An experiment that disproved an ancient dictum and gave birth to the barometer.

Aristotle, the greatest scientist of antiquity, said that nature abhors a vacuum – so that's what people believed in the early 17th century when lift pumps were becoming popular. Nature would get rid of a vacuum by pushing water up the pipe of a pump to fill the empty space. By this reasoning water had to lift indefinitely as long as the pump worked. When someone pointed out to Galileo that a new pump could lift water to a height of only about ten metres, Galileo asked his pupil Torricelli to investigate the problem.

Due to the practical difficulties of experimenting with a long pipe, Torricelli came up with the bright idea of using a heavier liquid, mercury. As mercury is 13.5 times heavier than water, he expected that the maximum height which mercury could be lifted by a pump would be about 76 centimetres. He took a glass tube, about a metre long, sealed at one end. He filled it with mercury, placed his thumb over the open end, upturned the tube and then removed his thumb into a bowl of mercury. The mercury, which originally filled the whole tube, now stood to a height of 76 centimetres, leaving a vacuum above it. He suggested that the mercury column was supported by the atmospheric pressure and its height would vary slightly from day to day.

Torricelli's experiment disproved Aristotle, and his apparatus was, of course, the first barometer.

The cause of royal delight

1661
England

Robert Boyle (1627–91)

Boyle destroyed the ancient concept of the elements and gave the word its current meaning.

The publication in 1661 of Boyle's book, *The Sceptical Chymist*, marks the beginning of modern chemistry. As a result alchemy changed into chemistry. In this book he rejected the ages-old notion of four elements – earth, air, fire and water – and presented the first scientific definition of an element. He said that elements were 'certain primitive and simple, or perfectly unmingled bodies'. In other words, elements are one of the simplest components of matter, which could not be converted into anything simpler. He also said that elements were 'incapable of decomposition' – and added the prophetic – 'by any means with which we are now acquainted'. We are now, of course, acquainted with means to decompose elements into simpler substances such as neutrons and protons.

The famous English diarist Samuel Pepys records that King Charles II – who himself dabbled in science and had his own private laboratory – 'mightily laughed' when told that scientists were 'spending time only in weighing air'. The cause of royal delight was Boyle's experiments on mass, volume and pressure of gases that led to what we know today as Boyle's law.

Boyle was a member of a group of thinkers in England who met regularly for philosophical discussions. In 1662 the group, known as the Invisible College, was incorporated by the Royal Charter into the Royal Society and its members became Fellows. The history of science since then is closely connected with the Society.

A very pleasant amusement

Isaac Newton (1642–1727)

1666
England

Newton was the first to examine a colour spectrum produced by a prism.

> *Sir Isaac Newton was the boy*
> *That climbed the apple tree, sir;*
> *He then fell down and broke his crown*
> *And lost his gravity, sir.*

This amusing verse from J. A. Sidey's poem 'The Irish Schoolmaster' (1913) tells another version of the best-known anecdote in science. Not so well known is the story of Newton's prism. In 1666 he bought a triangular glass prism 'to try therewith the celebrated phenomena of colours'. He allowed a beam of sunlight to pass through a small round hole in a window shutter of a darkened room and placed the prism in the path of the beam. He was expecting a circle of white light on the opposite wall, and he was quite surprised to see instead a band of seven colours: red, orange, yellow, green, blue, indigo and violet. 'It was at first a very pleasant divertissement [amusement]', he wrote.

When he passed the spectrum through a second prism the seven colours were recombined into white light. Newton correctly suggested that white light is not homogenous, but is made up of different colours.

William Wordsworth refers to Newton's prism in this 1799 poem.

> *Where the statue stood*
> *Of Newton with his prism and silent face,*
> *The marble index of a mind for ever*
> *Voyaging through strange seas of Thought, alone.*

See also PHILOSOPHIAE NATURALIS PRINCIPIA MATHEMATICA, p. 38.

1669
Germany

The element of life and death

Hennig Brand (c. 1630–c. 1692)

Brand was the first recorded discoverer of an element that wasn't known in any form before.

The 19th-century Dutch physiologist Jakob Moleschott once said that without phosphorus there is no thought. This is true because nerve tissues contain phosphorus. It's also a constituent of DNA, meaning there's no life without phosphorus either.

Phosphorus was discovered by mere chance by Brand, a merchant and amateur alchemist. Like all other alchemists he was interested in finding the philosopher's stone – the mythical substance which, alchemists believed, could change base metals into gold. For years he dissolved, mixed, sieved and heated various acids, alkalis and minerals to form countless concoctions but the philosopher's stone remained elusive. One day it occurred to him that he might find it in urine. When he heated urine in a retort, a substance, white as snow, settled at the bottom. The waxy substance wouldn't change iron into gold but it still had an aura of mystery about it. It glowed eerily in the dark, so brightly that Brand could read his ancient alchemy books by it.

Brand sold some of the phosphorus to a Daniel Kraft who made a lot of money by demonstrating its fascinating glow to the courts of Europe. Kraft passed a sample on to the English chemist Robert Boyle who succeeded in preparing it and published the first book on its chemistry, *The Aerial Noctiluca* (1680). Phosphorus was the favourite of poisoners in the 18th and 19th centuries. Once ingested it was impossible to detect by the forensic scientists of the day.

'Little animalcules'

Anton van Leeuwenhoek (1632–1723)

1677
Holland

Leeuwenhoek was the first human being to see micro-organisms.

The Microbe is so very small
You cannot make him out at all
But many sanguine people hope
To see him down a microscope.

So writes Hilaire Belloc in *More Beasts for Worse Children* (1897). The first 'sanguine person' to see microbes or micro-organisms down a microscope was Leeuwenhoek, a draper and haberdasher. He did not invent the microscope (it was invented in *c.* 1590 by Dutch spectacle maker Hans Janssen and his son Zacharias) but made hundreds of microscopes with his own hands. His most powerful microscope had a magnification of about x 300.

Before 1677, the smallest creatures known were cheese mites, which are just visible to the naked eye. Van Leeuwenhoek first discovered something smaller – what he called 'little animalcules' – in a drop of water, viewed through a microscope. In a letter to the Royal Society of London he described his remarkable find as 'so exceedingly small that millions of millions might be contained in a drop of water' and called them 'the most wretched creatures that I have ever seen'. He was observing protozoa.

Over 50 years he wrote about 200 letters to the Society describing his findings. When he took up this hobby he was already 40 and had no scientific training, but his letters include descriptions so detailed and minute that bacteriologists can identify many micro-organisms just by reading them. Such was his output that scientists took a century to digest his pioneering work.

1687
England

The book that changed the world's view of the universe

Isaac Newton (1642–1727)

Known as the *Principia*, Newton's work is generally considered the greatest scientific book ever written.

Written in Latin, Book 1 of *Principia* states Newton's three laws of motion and presents the general principles of mechanics. Book 2 deals with the motion of fluids. Book 3 introduces the concept of gravity.

It took Newton eighteen months to write his magnum opus. 'For eighteen months Newton seldom left his rooms in Trinity, unconscious whether or not he had eaten his meals, and taking little time for sleep', notes British science historian A. E. E. McKenzie. 'He would spend whole days sitting on his bed, half-dressed, thinking.' Newton's absent-mindedness was legendary. Irish poet Thomas Moore relates a handed-down story in his *Journal* (1820s): 'He insisted that his breakfast egg must cook exactly five minutes; on one occasion the maid entered the kitchen to find Newton before the stove, thoughtfully looking at the egg, which rested in his hand, while his watch lay in the saucepan of boiling water.'

The *Principia* guided the development of modern physics. However, Einstein revised many of Newton's ideas. Alexander Pope's famous couplet (*c.* 1732) relates:

> *Nature, and Nature's laws, lay hid in night.*
> *God said, 'Let Newton be!' and all was light.*

And in 1926, J. C. Squire replied:

> *It did not last: the Devil howling 'Ho,*
> *Let Einstein be!', restored the status quo.*

See also COLOUR SPECTRUM, p. 35.

Degrees of difference

Ole Rømer (1644–1710)

1700
Denmark

Rømer was the first to devise a scale to measure degrees of temperature.

The ancient civilisations had learned to measure the three fundamental quantities – mass, length and time. But they didn't know of any device for measuring temperature. They could only use words like hot and cold. In 1592 Galileo made the first instrument for measuring temperature – an air thermometer.

In 1700 Rømer, an astronomer who is best known for the first measurement of the speed of light, also invented the liquid-in-glass thermometer, which used a mixture of water and alcohol. He devised a quantitative temperature scale for his thermometer, with the boiling point of water at 60° and freezing point at 7.5° (he chose this number so that one-eighth of his scale would be below the freezing point; at that time scientists erroneously believed that the coldest possible temperature 0° was that of a mixture of ice and salt). So why don't we read temperatures in °R today? He never bothered to publish his scale, leaving this path open for others following him.

In 1714 Gabriel Fahrenheit, a German instrument maker who had visited Rømer in 1708, made the first mercury-in-glass thermometer. He set the boiling point at 96° (changed to 212°F after his death) and the freezing point at 32°. In 1742 the Swede Anders Celsius, another astronomer tired of observing the heavens, decided to devise his own temperature scale. After a series of meticulous experiments, he fixed the boiling point at 0° and the freezing point at 100°. After his death, scientists reversed the two figures. For trivia fans: the Fahrenheit and Celsius readings are the same at −40°.

Counting in 0s and 1s

Gottfried Leibniz (1646–1716)

The binary system of notation is a base-2 system that represents numeric values using only the symbols 0 and 1.

This means that binary numbers are much longer than decimal equivalents (for example, decimal 9 is binary 1001, and decimal 90 is binary 1011010), but they use the same arithmetic rules as decimal numbers. Binary numbers are simple to use; there are no multiplication tables to memorise.

The famous biographer of mathematicians, E. T. Bell, calls Leibniz a 'master of all trades' ('"Jack of all trades, master of none" has spectacular exceptions like any other folk proverb, and Leibniz, is one of them'). Leibniz was a mathematician and philosopher contemporary to Newton. They both developed calculus independently; however, the terminology and notation of calculus we know today is due to Leibniz. He also introduced many other mathematical symbols: the decimal point, the equal sign, the colon (:) for division and ratio, and the dot for multiplication.

It's believed that Leibniz developed the binary system for use in philosophical arguments on religion where 1 represented God and 0 an absence of God. *Binary* is the Latin word for 'two at a time'. The system was ignored by his contemporaries because it had no practical application. But it came into widespread use when the first digital computers were invented in the 1940s. Digital computers process data in binary numbers. Binary numbers are useful in computers because 0 and 1 can be represented in many ways; for example, by on or off lamps, open or closed switches, or black or white dots on the screen.

Great balls of fire

Edmond Halley (1656–1742)

1705
England

Comets follow predictable orbits, cycles and returns.

The awe-inspiring spectacle of a comet has always intrigued people. Its irregular appearance in the sky, its varying size, form and brightness, its exotic tail, its abrupt disappearance; these were the mysteries which ancient people were unable to solve. To them comets were omens of disaster. Comets are no longer considered harbingers of doom, but they still intrigue astronomers. Even now, astronomers know much about comets and yet they still can't predict when the next one will come. But once they spot a comet, they can predict its orbit, cycle and return, thanks to Halley.

Halley, an astronomer, was a friend of Newton and helped him publish *Principia* (see p. 38). When young Halley observed a bright comet in 1682, he calculated its orbit. He decided to study the orbits of other previously observed comets. When he delved into historical records he was amazed to find an account of a bright comet in 1607 studied by Kepler, and other accounts of comets in 1531, 1456, 1380 and 1305. They all appeared roughly every 75 years and travelled in the same part of the sky as the comet of 1682.

He spent several years calculating orbits of comets in relation to other heavenly bodies, and in 1705 published his findings in a book, *A Synopsis of the Astronomy of Comets.* He successfully predicted that the comet of 1682 would return in 1758. This comet now bears Halley's name and is the most famous of all comets. It was last seen in 1986, and is expected to return in 2061.

Males are from Mars, females are from Venus

Carlolus Linnaeus (1707–78)

Linnaeus introduced the symbols ♂ and ♀ for the male and female genders.

Linnaeus was the first to classify species. He proposed a binomial nomenclature in which each species was given a Latin name consisting of two parts: the genus name, which comes first and begins with a capital letter, and the species name, which begins with a lower-case letter (for example, *Homo sapiens*). The system is still used today.

Linnaeus's classification of plants was based on their sexual organs. Not only were plants sexed, they actually became 'husbands' and 'wives'. Their sex lives reflected 18th-century values. 'If male and female flowers occurred on the same plant, they shared the same house (monoecia) but not the same bed; if on separate plants, they lived in two houses (*dioecia*). Hermaphroditic flowers [with both male and female reproductive organs] contained husbands and wives in one bed (*monoclinia*)', notes Londa Schiebinger, an American historian. Linnaeus also turned the alchemists' symbols for 'hard' iron (δ, delta, from the ancient Greek symbol for Mars) and 'soft' copper (φ, phi, for Venus) into ♂ and ♀.

Erasmus Darwin, grandfather of Charles, was a physician and poet. He translated some of Linnaeus's works. His 250-couplet poem *The Loves of Plants* (1789) personifies 90 species to instruct the reader in the Linnaean system. A sample:

> *Sweet blooms Genista in myrtle shade,*
> *And ten fond brothers woo the haughty maid.*

(Meaning: the flower of Genista or broom has ten males, stamens, and one female, pistil)

A bolt from the blue

Benjamin Franklin (1706–90)

1752
USA

Franklin's kite experiment, the most famous experiment in the annals of science, showed the electrical nature of lightning.

Lightning is the electrical discharge between clouds and the Earth. The friction of moving air during a thunderstorm builds an electric charge within a cloud, making the top of the cloud positive and the bottom negative. Most of the charge is lost within the cloud, but if the negative charge is high, it leaks to the positively charged ground below. This creates a bolt of visible lightning.

For his experiment, Franklin used a silk kite with a wire at the tip of the cross; an iron key at the bottom of the string; and a silk ribbon tied on to this. He could fly the kite safely by holding the ribbon. The string became wet in the thunderstorm and charge passed from the kite to the key.

Franklin was a printer before he became famous as a scientist and politician. He wrote the following epitaph for himself, but it was never used.

The body of
Benjamin Franklin, printer
(Like the covers of an old book,
Its contents worn out,
And strippt of its leathering and gilding)
Lies here, food for worms!
Yet the work itself shall not be lost,
For it will, as he believed, appear once more,
In a new
And more beautiful edition,
Corrected and amended
By its author.

That tingly sensation

Joseph Priestley (1733–1804)

1767
England

Soda water, or carbonated water, is water into which carbon dioxide gas has been dissolved.

Priestley never studied science formally but he is remembered for a stream of chemical discoveries. He was a skilful experimenter and many of his experiments took place at a brewery adjacent to his house. Carbon dioxide gas is produced during beer making and, as it's much heavier than air, most of it settles above the surface of the fermenting liquid. In one of his experiments on 'fixed air', as carbon dioxide was known then, Priestley took two jars: one full of water and the other empty. He held the empty jar upside down over the liquid for a while and then poured water into it from the other jar. Some of the gas was dissolved in water. By repeating the process a few times he had created the pleasant sparkling drink we now call soda water.

Priestley's discovery started a craze for this new drink, which was believed to possess healing properties. Carbon dioxide when dissolved into water produces a very weak carbonic acid, which – although it doesn't add any health benefits – is what causes the tingly sensation on your tongue. And when a bottle of soda water is opened, it's carbon dioxide gas that produces the familiar fizz.

Adding various flavours and sugar to soda water turns it into fizzy soft drinks. If Priestley – who was awarded the Royal Society's coveted Copley Medal for his discovery – hadn't hovered over beer vats for so long, perhaps we wouldn't worry today about 'unhealthy' soft drinks.

When the sack hit the ceiling

Joseph Black (1728–99)

1767
Scotland

Since hydrogen gas is lighter than air, a hydrogen-filled balloon displaces air. This creates buoyancy (the upward force) which lifts the balloon.

Black is known to science students for the discovery of latent heat and specific heat, not as a pioneer of hydrogen balloons. That honour is reserved for Jacques Charles, the French scientist famous for Charles's Law. In 1767 Black performed an experiment in which he filled a sack with 'inflammable air', as hydrogen gas was then known, and released it. To the amazement of his audience, which included many scientists, the sack floated to the ceiling. The audience accused him of an elaborate hoax involving thin black thread. This sack trick led to the development of hydrogen balloons. In 1783 Charles designed a large hydrogen-filled balloon which ascended over Paris to a height of about 900 metres. By the end of that year hydrogen and hot air balloons were being used for carrying passengers.

Black was a professor of chemistry at Edinburgh. In those days students paid their admission fees directly to their professors. As cutting tiny pieces from gold coins was common practice, on admission days Black sat at the entrance of the hall with a balance on a table at his side. He weighed all coins and rejected the ones that weren't full weight. He calculated that he might have lost as much as 50 guineas every year by accepting 'light' coins. He was not a miser but a stickler for accuracy.

Today gas-filled balloons are mainly used for high-altitude scientific or meteorological research.

1775
Austria

'Ninety per cent gobbledygook'

Franz Mesmer (1734–1815)

Mesmer claimed that this bogus therapy cured illnesses through the invisible forces of 'animal magnetism' that flow through our bodies.

Mesmer, a physician who got his doctorate for a thesis on how the gravity of various planets affects health, proposed that an invisible magnetic field flows through our bodies. If the flow were restricted somehow, it would cause physical and mental illnesses. He theorised that by passing magnets over the body, the fluid would be unblocked and the patient cured. He managed to cure some patients by this method. He eventually discovered that he could achieve the same results by the passing of hands over the body. He claimed that he was now making use of 'animal magnetism'.

In 1778 he moved to Paris where he became quite the rage. He would ask his patients to sit with their feet in a tub filled with 'magnetised water' while holding iron rods attached to the tub. He would than emerge from behind heavy drapes dressed in purple silk and holding an iron rod. This showmanship infuriated Parisians so much that in 1784 King Louis XVI instituted a scientific enquiry into 'animal magnetism'. The enquiry concluded that the observed effects could be attributed to the power of suggestion (a kind of placebo effect) and that the practice was nothing but 'the art of increasing the imagination by degrees'.

The well-known science writer Isaac Asimov says that Mesmer was 'ninety percent gobbledygook'. Anyway, he is immortalised in the phrases 'animal magnetism' and 'mesmerise' (for example, 'his roguish animal magnetism mesmerised her') and his cure survives in New Age magnetic therapies.

God exists, so does Sudoku

1776
Russia

Leonhard Euler (1707–83)

**A completed grid of the popular puzzle Sudoku is a
Latin square.**

In a magic square, the numbers in all the rows, columns and diagonals of the matrix add up to the same sum; while in a Latin square, cells are filled with n numbers (or symbols) so that no row or column contains the same number twice and each number is used precisely n times. The origin of the Latin square dates back to medieval times. Euler was the first mathematician to study them systematically and call them Latin squares.

A Sudoku-like puzzle, called the Number Place, first appeared in the United States in 1979. The puzzle was subsequently introduced in Japan in 1984 where it was christened Sudoku ('single numbers' in Japanese). In 1997 Wayne Gould, a New Zealander and retired judge living in Hong Kong, was mesmerised when he saw a partially completed puzzle in a Japanese bookshop. He spent six years writing a computer program that automatically generates Sudoku grids. In 2004 the London *Times* introduced the puzzle in its pages and the rest is history.

Swiss-born Euler became totally blind in 1766 but that didn't diminish his mathematical productivity. He was invited by Catherine the Great to live in St Petersburg. The story goes that she asked Euler to silence the visiting French philosopher Denis Diderot, who was trying to convert her courtiers to atheism. Euler said gravely to Diderot: 'Sir, $a + b^n / n = x$, hence God exists; reply.' The mathematically challenged philosopher was speechless.

1781
England

Astronomical ardour finds a new planet

William Herschel (1738–1822)

The discovery of Uranus was the first recorded discovery of a planet in human history.

Herschel, a trained musician, became interested in astronomy when he was an organist at the fashionable Octagon Chapel in the city of Bath. The art of making telescopes fascinated him and he made his own telescopes, while his younger sister Caroline helped him in his observations. According to Robert Ball in *The Great Astronomers* (1895), Caroline complained that in his 'astronomical ardour he sometimes omitted to take off, before going into his workshop, the beautiful lace ruffles which he wore while conducting a concert, and consequently they became soiled with the pitch employed in the polish of his mirrors'.

On the evening of 13 March 1781, Herschel was surveying the sky from his telescope when he came across an object that appeared to be more than an ordinary star. He applied a higher magnifying power to examine it closely. The object seemed like a tiny yellow-green disk. When he looked at it again after a few days, he found it had moved from its original position. The organist had discovered the seventh planet. Mercury, Venus, Earth, Mars, Jupiter and Saturn have been known since ancient times.

This excerpt from Alfred Noyes's 1922 epic poem, *The Torch-Bearers*, describes Herschel's thoughts.

> *My periwig's askew, my ruffle stained*
> *With grease from my new telescope!*
> > *Ach, to-morrow*
> *How Caroline will be vexed, although she grows*
> *Almost as bad as I, who cannot leave*
> *My workshop for one evening.*

48

Discovering H$_2$O

Henry Cavendish (1731–1810)

1784
England

Cavendish synthesised water from hydrogen and oxygen.

In the 18th century many scientists believed that water was an element. In 1784 Cavendish, an eccentric aristocrat and a superb scientist who had discovered hydrogen in 1766, placed hydrogen and oxygen in a eudiometer (a strong glass tube closed at one end, in which two wires are placed to conduct an electric spark). When he exploded the two gases by passing an electrostatic discharge from a Leyden jar (a device that produces sparks of electricity) into the eudiometer, he found that oxygen and twice its volume of hydrogen had combined to form pure water.

Cavendish, who has been called 'the richest of all learned men and the most learned of all rich men' by Jean Baptiste Biot, a contemporary French scientist, was shy and uncomfortable in the presence of strangers. He 'probably uttered fewer words in the course of his life than any man who ever lived to 80 years, not at all excepting the monks of La Trappe', according to Lord Brougham, a contemporary British writer and politician. He usually communicated with his housekeeper by leaving written instructions on a table in the hall. His library was in a London mansion a few miles from his residence. Everyone was allowed to borrow from the library as long as they left a proper receipt. He himself would sign a formal receipt for all the books he took with him.

Cavendish's experiment gave a deathblow to the centuries-old idea that water was an element.

1790
France

Litre's daughter called Millie

A commission of 28 scientists appointed by the
French Academy

The metric system is based on the decimal (base-10) system.

In the late 18th century, science in France was developing faster than anywhere else in the world, but the French employed more units than any other country. For length, for example, they had the *foot*, the *inch*, the *toise* (6 feet) and the *line* ($\frac{1}{12}$ inch). In the middle of the French Revolution, the French Academy appointed a commission which standardised the units of length, weight and volume and named them *metre*, *gram* and *litre*. The units became official in 1799.

The metric system we use today is known as the SI (Système International) and was introduced in 1960. Many SI units are named after scientists, but litre is definitely not named after the fictional 'French scientist Claude Émile Jean Baptiste Litre (1716–78)'. In 1978, *Chem 13 News*, a Canadian chemistry newsletter, published a 'biography' of 'Litre' suggesting that 'in celebration of the 200th anniversary of the death of this great scientist, it has been decided to use his name for the SI unit of volume (the abbreviation will be L, following the standard practice of using capital letters for units named after scientists)'. The spoof turned into a literary hoax when a précis of the article appeared in the newsletter of the prestigious International Union of Pure and Applied Chemistry. The spoof also fooled many other publications and radio programmes. But most scientists got the joke. Some joined in the fun, creating a daughter for Litre, named Millie.

The SI is now used widely, except in the United States.

The frog's dancing master

Luigi Galvani (1737–98)

1791
Italy

Electricity is produced in the moist tissues of animals, says Galvani's erroneous theory.

There are various accounts of the story of how the twitching leg of a dead frog led Galvani, professor of anatomy at the University of Bologna, to his famous theory of 'animal electricity'. According to one version, the physician had recommended a soup of frogs' legs for his sick wife Lucia. He decided to cook it himself. He cut up some frogs and suspended their legs by copper hooks on an iron balcony of his house. He was astonished to note that the legs shook convulsively every time they chanced to touch the iron of the balcony.

He repeated the experiment in his laboratory. He observed that leg muscles of a frog contracted when they were touched with two different metals. In another experiment, he passed the discharge from a Leyden jar, a contemporary device for storing static electricity, through the leg of a frog, and observed spasmodic contraction in the muscles. He tried a further series of experiments and finally concluded that he had discovered 'animal electricity'. He expounded the wrong theory that the muscles of frogs were the source of electricity. When his essay, 'Treatise on the Force of Animal Electricity as Exerted upon Muscular Movement', appeared in 1791, he was laughed at as 'the frog's dancing master'.

Galvani had in fact made the first primitive battery in which electric current could be produced by two different metals in a suitable solution, but blundered when he tried to explain the source of the current.

See also ELECTRIC BATTERY, p. 57.

Stones from the heavens

1794
Germany

Ernst Chladni (1756–1827)

Meteorites are remnants of geological processes that formed our solar system about 4.6 billion years ago, but in Chladni's time the idea that meteorites were extraterrestrial in origin was scientific heresy.

In his book *On the Origin of Iron-masses*, Chladni claimed that stones and masses of iron fall from the sky and some of them even create fireballs in the atmosphere. He suggested that these objects originated in 'cosmic space' and might be remnants of planet formation or planetary debris from explosions or collisions.

Scientists at the time mocked Chladni's idea. They considered it an attack on the great Newton himself, who believed that apart from the heavenly bodies – stars, planets and comets – all space beyond the Moon was empty (the heavens are empty of all matter except a very thin, invisible ether, he said in 1704). Georg C. Lichtenberg 'wished Chladni had not written his book'. He felt that Chladni had been 'hit on the head with one of his stones'.

When a spectacular shower of several thousand stones fell near the town of L'Aigle in northern France in 1803, the French scientist Jean Baptiste Biot investigated the phenomenon. Biot's report finally convinced the scientific establishment that stones do fall from the heavens. Most meteorites are pieces of rock and/or metal from asteroids (see p. 58); but most meteors (also known as falling or shooting stars because they leave momentary streaks of light in the sky) are produced when comets disintegrate. Chladni is now remembered as the founder of meteoritics, the science of meteorites.

See also THREAT FROM METEORITES, p. 156.

Country wisdom

Edward Jenner (1749–1823)

1796
England

Injection of a vaccine (killed or weakened micro-organisms) in order to provide immunity against a particular disease.

In the 18th century smallpox was the most dreadful infectious disease. Its victims, if they survived, were usually left severely disfigured, with deep pockmarks scarring the skin. As a young apprentice doctor, Jenner heard milkmaids saying that they couldn't be infected by smallpox since they had already had cowpox. Cowpox is a mild disease which causes minor sores on udders of cows, and anyone infected with it develops sores on their hands. Many years later, Jenner – now a qualified doctor in Gloucestershire – recalled this incident. He decided to test whether there was any truth to this country wisdom.

In 1796 he took some fluid from the sore of a milkmaid suffering from cowpox and injected the fluid in the arms of a healthy eight-year-old boy – such an experiment would be illegal today! Seven weeks later Jenner infected the boy with some fluid taken from the sore of a person suffering from smallpox. The boy did not show any symptoms of smallpox. Cowpox had given him immunity from smallpox. After tests on several other children, including his own eleven-month-old son, Jenner published his findings in 1798. He called the process vaccination (from the Latin *vacca*, cow). Vaccination soon spread throughout the world, but the immediate reaction to it was ridicule. In 1802 James Gillray, a famous caricaturist, published a cartoon that showed 'various whimsical results' of vaccination, such as people sprouting cows' heads.

In 1980 the World Health Organization declared the planet free of smallpox.

1798
Austria

Reading 'bumps' on the head

Franz Gall (1758–1828)

Phrenology, a pseudoscience, is the study of the shape and size of the head to determine a person's character and mental abilities.

In 1798, Gall, a physician, wrote to a friend:

> I have at last the pleasure of presenting you my treatise on the functions of the brain … to show that it is possible by observing various elevations and depressions on the surface of the head to determine the degrees of different aspects of the personality. This work will be of the first importance to medicine, morality, education and the law – indeed to the whole science of human nature.

The ten-page letter, which was published in a German journal, marked the beginning of phrenology.

Gall made two major assertions. First, he believed that different mental functions are located in different parts of the brain, called organs. He identified 27 discrete organs of behaviour. If you move your finger on the back of your neck, you will notice a bump formed by the base of your skull. This bump, according to Gall, marked the location of the Organ of Amativeness, the organ that linked to sexual arousal. Second, he argued that the growth of the various organs is related to the development of associated mental faculties. As this growth would be reflected in the shape of the skull, personality traits could be determined by reading 'bumps' on the skull.

Phrenology is, of course, nonsense, but in the early 19th century it was a respected science. People sought the advice of phrenologists not only for diagnosing mental illness, but for hiring employees, or even selecting marriage partners.

See also APHASIA, p. 75.

'Fancy such a bright colour'

John Dalton (1766–1844)

Dalton was the first to investigate colour blindness, a genetic defect of colour perception.

The story goes that Dalton gave his mother a pair of stockings as a birthday present. 'You have bought me a very fine pair of stockings, but what made you fancy such a bright colour?' she asked. 'I can never show myself at meetings in them. They're as red as cherry, John.' Much distressed by his mother's remark, he asked his elder brother who, like Dalton, thought the stockings were a drab darkbluish colour. When their neighbours also remarked 'very fine stuff, but uncommon scarlety', Dalton realised that he and his brother suffered from some genetic defect.

Dalton, known for his atomic theory and the law of partial pressures, made the first scientific study of colour blindness. He published the details of his investigation in a paper entitled 'Extraordinary Facts Relating to the Vision of Colours'. A humble and frugal man, Dalton was highly admired by his contemporaries. When he died, the City of Manchester decided to give its famous citizen a state funeral. His body was viewed by more than 40,000 persons. The funeral procession was made up of more than 100 horse carriages and countless people on foot.

Colour blindness – called *le Daltonisme* in French – is caused by a deficiency in photoreceptors, a fact Dalton didn't discover (he thought the insides of his eyeballs were blue). Complete colour blindness is a rare disease. Red–green blindness affects about 8 per cent of the male population, but is quite rare in females.

Maybe

1799
France

Pierre Simon Laplace (1749–1827)

Can we predict the future, or is it arbitrary and random?

Laplace, a mathematician, believed that nature follows exact laws and if an 'omniscient calculator' knew the positions and speeds of all the particles in the universe, it would be able to calculate their positions and speeds at any time in the future. This principle is known as scientific determinism. Newton's laws support the deterministic view of the universe. In the early 20th century the new field of quantum mechanics – which deals with the behaviour of nature at atomic level – suggested that the events at atomic level occur randomly. This introduced the idea of indeterminism or unpredictability.

After the publication of the first two volumes of his five-volume *Mécanique céleste* ('Celestial Mechanics'), Laplace went to see Napoleon Bonaparte to present a copy. Someone had told Napoleon that the book contained no mention of the name of God. Napoleon received the book with the remark: 'You have written this large book on the system of the universe without once mentioning its Creator.' Laplace replied bluntly: 'Sire, I have no need of that hypothesis.'

Einstein thought that the universe was deterministic in some ways. He was fond of saying: 'God does not play dice with the universe.' Once Niels Bohr retorted: 'Who are you to tell God what to do?' And Stephen Hawking has added his own wisdom: 'God sometimes throws dice where they can't be seen.' The dicey debate continues.

Napoleon receives an electric shock

1800
Italy

Alessandro Volta (1745–1827)

The voltaic pile battery was the first device that could produce electricity continuously.

When Volta, professor of natural philosophy at the University of Padua, read of his fellow countryman Galvani's experiment (see p. 51), he tried it himself and remarked that he had 'swung over from incredulity to enthusiastic belief'. But he disagreed with the theory of 'animal electricity'. He suspected that the current was produced somehow by two metals, copper and iron, not the frogs' legs. After experimenting for eight years, Volta found the answer when he dipped discs of copper and zinc in a bowl of salt solution and obtained a continuous supply of electric current. His simple device was different from Leyden jars which stored electricity produced by electrostatic machines and were capable of generating only a single discharge.

He reasoned that a much larger charge could be produced by stacking several discs separated by discs of flannel soaked in salt water. By attaching wires to each end of the 'pile' he successfully obtained a steady current. The 'voltaic pile' was the first battery in history. In 1800 he described his experiment in a letter to the Royal Society of London.

A year later Napoleon Bonaparte invited him to Paris to demonstrate his invention. The battery gave a mild shock when the top disc was touched by one hand and the bottom one with the other. The demonstration was attended by prominent French scientists, and everyone, including Napoleon, tried the trick. Whenever you use the word 'volt' remember it honours the scientist who 'shocked' Napoleon.

1801
Italy

A new century's gift

Giuseppe Piazzi (1746–1826)

Ceres was the first asteroid discovered.

On the evening of 1 January 1801, Piazzi, a monk and director of the Palermo Observatory, pointed his telescope at stars in the constellation Taurus and observed an unfamiliar faint object. He thought he'd discovered a new planet orbiting between Mars and Jupiter. He named it Ceres Ferdinandea (Ceres for the patron goddess of Sicily, and Ferdinandea for his royal patron, King Ferdinand of Naples and Sicily), declaring: 'I have the full right to name it in the most convenient way to me, like something I own. I will always use the name Ceres Ferdinandea, nor by giving it another name will I suffer to be reproached for ingratitude towards Sicily and its king.' The name was soon as shortened to Ceres.

The discovery of Ceres posed a problem for astronomers: it was too small to be a planet. In 1802 the British astronomer William Herschel suggested that Ceres represented a new class of celestial bodies. He proposed that they should be called 'asteroids' (from the Greek *asteroeidēs*, 'starlike').

Astronomers now know of about 200 asteroids with a diameter larger than 100 kilometres and 800 larger than 30 kilometres. About a million are a kilometre or more across; and billions are of boulder or pebble size. Most of the asteroids orbit within a vast, doughnut-shaped ring between Mars and Jupiter, known as the main belt. Occasionally, a collision kicks an asteroid out of the belt, sending it onto a dangerous path that crosses Earth's orbit. It's these Earth-crossers that pose a threat to our planet (see p. 156).

See also ASTEROID SATELLITES, p. 188.

Little white sugar pills

Samuel Hahnemann (1755–1843)

1810
Germany

Is homeopathy, one of the most popular complementary therapies, a medical breakthrough or a major blunder in the history of medicine?

While translating a medical textbook into German, Hahnemann, a qualified physician, was puzzled by a passage that described the treatment of malaria by quinine. At that time, no one knew how quinine worked. He decided to experiment with quinine by taking it himself. The drug produced symptoms very similar to those of malaria. Fascinated by this discovery, he started testing other drugs to determine the types of symptoms they produced. To make them safer, he diluted them in alcohol. He was amazed to find that the more dilute a solution was, the stronger its effects.

From his limited observations, which themselves were based on the folk medicine of the day, he came up with the theory 'like cures like'. To describe his method of healing he coined the word homeopathy (from the Greek words *homoios* and *patheia*, meaning 'suffering'). He published his new system of medicine in *Organon of Rational Art of Healing* (1810), which is still used today as a basic text of homeopathy.

There's no scientific evidence supporting homeopathy's principle that a disease can be treated by giving patients ultra-dilute doses of a medicine that would in healthy persons produce symptoms similar to those of the disease. Most large clinical trials have conclusively shown that homeopathic remedies are no better than placebos. If they seem to work, it's because the mind can affect the body's biochemistry.

A to Z of spectrum

1812
Germany

Joseph von Fraunhofer (1787–1826)

Fraunhofer lines are the dark lines in the Sun's spectrum.

The emission or absorption spectrum of a substance is its finger-print. An emission spectrum has bright lines on a black background; it's produced when a substance gives off light when it is excited by heating or by passing a large electric current through it. An absorption spectrum is a spectrum with dark lines in it; it's produced when light is passed through a gas or a liquid, or strikes a solid.

In 1802, nearly a century and a half after Newton studied the spectrum, the English scientist William Wollaston observed seven dark lines in the Sun's spectrum. Ten years later Fraunhofer, an optical instrument maker, detected nearly 700 lines. He accurately measured these lines, and labelled the prominent ones with the letters A to Z, a nomenclature still used today. However, he never provided any explanation for them. That came in 1860 from the later German scientists, Robert Bunsen (of Bunsen burner fame) and Gustav Kirchhoff (famous for his laws of electric circuits), who showed that each chemical element produces its own characteristic lines in its spectrum of light.

The dark lines in the spectrum of the Sun – and other stars – are caused by the absorption of particular wavelengths by cooler gas layers of the Sun's atmosphere. These lines (modern physicists can find more than 25,000 lines) are now called Fraunhofer lines. Fraunhofer, who was scorned as a mere instrument maker by contemporary scientists, pioneered how scientists identify elements in stars.

The language of chemistry

Jöns Berzelius (1779–1848)

1814
Sweden

Berzelius rejected the old symbols of chemistry and introduced the modern system of chemical shorthand.

The early chemists expressed their chemical thoughts in strange symbols of alchemy. To ancient philosophers, the circle was the symbol of perfection. Alchemists used it as a symbol for gold, the perfect metal. Similarly, their other symbols were based on ancient myths and legends. In 1787 the French Academy of Sciences suggested using simple geometrical characters for gases, metals, alkalis and acids. To the English chemist John Dalton, who revived the idea of the atom as a unit of matter in 1808, atoms were solid spherical particles. He used circles to represent atoms: a circle for oxygen, a solid circle for carbon, a circle around S for silver, and so on.

These hieroglyphics created confusion because not every student of chemistry was a draftsperson. In 1814 the Swedish government put Berzelius in charge of compiling the new Swedish Pharmaco-poeia. 'The chemical sign ought to be letters for the greater facility of writing, and not disfigure a printed book', he declared. 'I shall therefore take for the chemical sign, the initial letter of the Latin name of each chemical element. If the first two letters be common in two elements I shall use both the initial letter and the first letter they have not in common.' He suggested joining the symbols of the elements to show compounds.

Dalton clung to his own system: 'Berzelius' symbols are horrify-ing. A young student might as soon learn Hebrew as make himself acquainted with them.' Students today would disagree.

'A law of great simplicity'

Georg Ohm (1789–1854)

This basic law of electricity simply states $V = IR$.

Ohm was a teacher of mathematics and science in a high school when he started his experiments on current electricity. At that time current electricity was a qualitative study and there were no accurate ways to measure various electrical quantities. From his experiments he established that the flow of electricity in a conductor depends upon its length, its cross-sectional area, and the material of which it's composed. He provided accurate definitions of voltage across a conductor (V), the current flowing through it (I) and its resistance (R) and the relationship between them, which is now known as Ohm's law.

When published in 1827, his treatise was badly received. A critic even called it 'the result of an incurable delusion'. Education authorities declared him 'unworthy to teach science' and forced him to resign from his school. His luck changed in 1833 when he was appointed a professor of physics. In 1841 the Royal Society of London honoured him for the discovery of his now famous law. He achieved 'nominal immortality' when in 1881 the unit of resistance was named after him. James D. Livingston, an American physicist, reminds us:

> So a fellow named Ohm with a felicity
> Dreamed up a law of great simplicity
> V equals IR
> Is what made Ohm a star
> It's a basic law of electricity.

'Bat-men' of the Moon

Richard Adams Locke (1800–71)

1835
USA

A famous British astronomer had discovered intelligent life on the Moon, claimed an elaborate hoax.

On 25 August 1835 a New York newspaper, *The Sun*, ran a front-page story with the headline 'GREAT ASTRONOMICAL DISCOVERIES LATELY MADE BY SIR JOHN HERSCHEL'. The story, purporting to be a reprint from a supplement of the *Edinburgh Journal of Science*, described fantastic sights of the Moon viewed by Herschel from his new telescope at the Cape of Good Hope. The story, which continued in instalments over the course of a few days, described the lunar landscape of vast forests, inland seas and lilac-hued 'very slender pyramids, standing in irregular groups, each composed of about thirty or forty spires'.

As *The Sun*'s sales soared from 8,000 to 19,360 copies its readers were introduced to *Vespertilio-homo* or 'bat-man' on the Moon: 'Certainly they were like human beings ... They averaged four feet in height, with short and glossy copper-colored hair and had wings composed of a thin membrane ...'

At the time of the publication of the articles, John Herschel, son of William (see p. 48) and one of the most famous scientists of his time, was in Cape Town surveying the southern skies. His only known comment is in a letter to his Aunt Caroline: 'I have been pestered from all quarters with that ridiculous hoax about the Moon – in English, French & German.' The author of the articles, the British-born journalist Locke, later claimed that the story was a satirical piece written to show the gullibility of Americans on the question of extraterrestrial life.

'I have seized the light'

1839
France

Louis Daguerre (1787–1851)

The first photographs, called daguerreotypes, were direct positive photographs.

Daguerre, an artist, became obsessed with the idea that he could make the image produced by the camera obscura a permanent one. The camera is essentially a box with a pinhole or lens in one end and a ground glass plate at the other end where the image is formed. Nicéphore Niépce, a fellow Frenchman who had improved the camera by fitting a movable lens in a tube to focus the image, was also interested in preserving the pictures. The two inventors formed a partnership, but Niépce died soon after. Daguerre continued to work alone exposing copper plates coated with light-sensitive silver iodide. All he got were faint pictures which faded quickly. One day he left an exposed plate in a cupboard full of various chemicals. When he took it out after a few days he was amazed to see a sharp, beautiful picture on the plate. After days of experiments he found the secret of his success: the plate had been developed by the mercury vapours from a broken bottle of mercury.

When he announced his discovery 'the people of Paris went nearly out of their minds with enthusiasm', describes Egon Larsen, the famous chronicler of the lives of inventors. 'There was a mad scramble to be "daguerreotyped". To sit for half an hour or longer in the pitiless sun, rigid and motionless, in order to take home a small metal plate with one's likeness on it – that was the latest fashion.'

'The art and craft of photography was born.'

The kitchen discovery that made tyres possible

1839
USA

Charles Goodyear (1800–60)

Vulcanisation is the treatment of rubber with sulphur or other chemicals to make it stronger and more elastic.

Natural rubber gets runny and sticky in the hot weather and turns stiff and brittle in very cold weather. Goodyear endured eight years of extreme hardship to find a process to make rubber stable. He ran into debts to feed his family and spent time in debtors' prison. Even while in prison he pursued his investigations with passion, asking his wife to bring him a lump of rubber, a rolling pin and some chemicals. With the permission of the humane prison superintendent he turned his prison cell into a laboratory. When he got out of the prison, he continued his experiments, which mainly involved kneading various chemicals into raw rubber.

One day he carelessly left a lump of rubber and some sulphur he'd used to treat it in the kitchen stove. Instead of melting, the rubber had turned into a gummy mass. 'As I was passing in and out of the room, I casually observed the little piece of gum which he was holding near the fire, and I noticed also that he was unusually animated by some discovery which he had made', his daughter recalled. 'He nailed the piece of gum outside the kitchen door in the intense cold. In the morning he brought it in, holding it up exultingly. He had found it perfectly flexible as it was when he put it out.' He patented the process in 1844. He died penniless; however, the future royalties made his family comfortable.

Vulcanisation (after Vulcan, the Roman god of fire) has changed the world by making tyres possible. Goodyear Tire Company was founded in 1898 long after Goodyear's death; it's not related in any way with Goodyear or his descendants though it honours his name.

Anaesthesia 'frolics'

1842
USA

Crawford Long (1815–78)

Ether was used as the first surgical anaesthetic.

Nitrous oxide is called 'laughing gas' because when inhaled it makes people feel happy. In the early 19th century, laughing gas 'frolics' at which guests breathed whiffs of gas were very popular. In 1844 Horace Wells, a dentist, attended one such party. He was surprised to see a youth who'd inhaled laughing gas stumbling against a bench, breaking his shins but feeling no pain. It suddenly occurred to him that laughing gas might work as a dental anaesthetic. Later he conducted a public demonstration of 'painless tooth extraction', but he administered too weak a dose of the gas, and the patient cried out of pain. The crowd jeered at him.

The credit for the first use of anaesthesia for surgical purposes goes to Long, a physician. He'd learned about ether during an 'ether frolic' (similar to the laughing-gas parties) at his medical school. He first tried it on his patients for minor operations. In 1842 he amputated a boy's toe painlessly, but didn't publish the results of this operation until 1849. In the meantime, William Morton, a student of Wells, performed the first tooth extraction with ether in 1846. The controversy about who discovered surgical anaesthesia continued until 1921, when the American College of Surgeons named Long the discoverer.

Ether and nitrous oxide have many harmful side effects and are no longer used as anaesthetics. Modern anaesthetics are very safe – and frolic-free.

Weaving algebraic patterns

1843
England

Ada Lovelace (1815–52)

Lovelace is generally acknowledged as the world's first computer programmer.

In 1834 Charles Babbage, an English mathematician and inventor, conceived an Analytical Engine, a device that had all the essential features of a modern computer: a separate store for holding numbers (memory), central 'mill' for working on them (processor) and a punched cards system for input and output. Though he prepared detailed designs and specifications for it, the Engine was never built. In 1842 Luigi Menabrea, a young engineer (later Italy's prime minister), published a paper on the Engine. Babbage asked his friend Lovelace, daughter of the poet Lord Byron, to translate the French edition of this paper into English. Lovelace not only translated the paper, but added a series of notes which were three times the length of the original paper.

In these notes she outlined the fundamental concepts of computer programming and wrote instructions for programming the calculations of the so-called Bernoulli numbers. 'We may say most aptly that the Analytical Engine weaves algebraic patterns just as the Jacquard-loom weaves flowers and leaves', she said in the notes. 'It does not occupy common ground with mere "calculating machines" … It has no pretensions whatever to originate any thing. It can do whatever we know how to order it to perform. It can follow analysis; but it has no power of anticipating any analytical relations or truths.'

Lovelace, the 'Enchantress of Numbers', as Babbage called her, effectively wrote the first computer program, but her program had no direct influence on the development of modern computer programming.

1845
Switzerland

Accidental kitchen chemistry

Christian Schönbein (1799–1868)

Nitrocellulose, or guncotton, is used in the manufacture of explosives and plastics.

German-born Schönbein, a professor of chemistry at the University of Basel, was a keen experimenter and would sometimes continue toying with chemicals – strictly against his wife's orders – in the kitchen. The story goes that one day, while his wife was absent, he was heating a mixture of nitric and sulphuric acids in a flask on the kitchen stove. He accidentally spilled some of the mixture over the bench. Terrified, he grabbed the first thing at hand, his wife's cotton apron, to mop up the spill, and then hung it over the stove to dry quickly. When it had dried enough, to Schönbein's amazement, the apron disappeared in a flash of flame, leaving no trace behind. The history of science doesn't record his wife's reaction to the disappearance of her apron, only that the timid professor had converted the cellulose of the apron into nitrocellulose, a smokeless explosive.

Schönbein also discovered ozone, a gas that's formed from oxygen in high-voltage electrical discharges in equipment such as photocopiers and laser printers. In the early 19th century, scientists were puzzled by the peculiar odour found near electrical equipment. In 1840 Schönbein traced this odour to a gas he named ozone (from the Greek *ozein*, 'to smell').

Despite his discoveries, he refused to accept the 'silly ideas' of atoms proposed by the English chemist John Dalton in 1808: 'If you can show me an atom as large as a liver dumpling, then perhaps I will believe in them. Perhaps.'

A sacred law that cannot be violated

1847
Germany

Hermann von Helmholtz (1821–94)

The law of conservation energy says that energy cannot be created or destroyed, but it may be changed from one form to another.

In 1842 the German physicist Julius Mayer proposed that energy 'once in existence cannot be annihilated, it can only change its form'. Five years later Helmholtz published his pamphlet 'On the Conservation of Forces' in which, independently of Mayer, he presented the law of conservation of energy in greater detail. He is usually given credit for its discovery.

Helmholtz was 26 and working in medicine when he published his physics pamphlet. An accomplished physician, physicist and philosopher, he was the most versatile scientist of his time. Even England's legendary magazine *Punch* was moved to publish an ode to him, which was reprinted in the journal *Nature* (1894).

> *What matter titles? Helmholtz is a name*
> *That challenges, alone, the award of Fame!*
> *When Emperors, Kings, Pretenders, shadows all,*
> *Leave not a dust-trace on our whirling ball,*
> *Thy work, oh grave-eyed searcher, shall endure,*
> *Unmarred by faction, from low passion pure.*

The law of conservation of energy (also called the first law of thermodynamics) is the most sacred law of physics. The law appeared shaky when Pauli tried to explain the radioactive decay of the nucleus (see p. 131), but it's faced no other challenges, at least so far.

Classes, lasses and asses

1848
Scotland

William Thomson (Lord Kelvin) (1824–1907)

The zero point of the absolute temperature scale is called absolute zero, the lowest temperature possible.

The triple point of a substance is the temperature and pressure at which the substance can exist in its three states at the same time – solid, liquid and gas. The triple point for water occurs at 0.01°C and 611.73 pascal. Thomson devised his own temperature scale based on the triple point of water. He used a 100-unit scale, like that in the Celsius scale, and by extrapolation arrived at –273° as the absolute zero point. In this scale, water freezes at 273° and boils at 373°.

The scale is now known as the Kelvin scale (symbol K without the degree sign) in honour of Thomson, and the absolute zero (0 K) has been refined to –273.15°C. However, no thermometer can be built to measure this temperature, where molecules have the lowest possible energy and the entropy (see p. 78) is zero.

Thomson, the greatest physicist of his time, became a professor at the University of Glasgow when he was 22 and remained there for more than half a century. One day he posted a notice on the door of his lecture room: 'Professor Thomson will not meet his classes today.' A mischievous student carefully erased 'c' from 'classes' and the notice now said: 'Professor Thomson will not meet his lasses today.' The next day, students, expecting mild rebuke from the professor, were amused to read the notice after the witty professor had removed one more letter: 'Professor Thomson will not meet his asses today.'

See also THIRD LAW OF THERMODYNAMICS, p. 102.

The colour purple

William Perkin (1838–1907)

1856

England

Mauve, a vibrant purple dye, was the first synthetic dye discovered.

Eighteen-year-old Perkin was crazy about chemistry and had his own laboratory at his home where he spent most of his evenings. He was interested in finding a method to synthesise the popular anti-malarial drug quinine. During his Easter holidays he mixed aniline, a chemical derived from coal tar, with potassium dichromate and noticed a black precipitate at the bottom of his beaker. He was about to pour out the worthless dregs – he was half expecting a colourless solution of quinine – when he noticed a purple tinge in the precipitate. He dissolved the black substance in alcohol and to his surprise it turned into a bright purple solution. He suspected that he had synthesised a new dye.

He sent a sample to a dyeing firm in Scotland. The reply came back: 'Your discovery is decidedly one of the most valuable that has come for a long time.' Perkin named the new compound 'mauve' and patented the process for making it. Mauve, a brilliant purple dye made from black coal tar, caught the imagination of Victorian England. 'It was the topic of conversation everywhere', notes a biographer, 'so much so that in a particular pantomime of the period, one of the characters, complaining of the way in which everyone would talk to him of nothing but mauve, added "Why even the policeman says to you *mauve* on there".'

Perkin built a dye factory and became immensely wealthy from a discovery he made by chance when he was only eighteen.

A topological conundrum

1858
Germany

Augustus Möbius (1790–1868)

A Möbius strip is a one-sided, one-edged continuous loop.

Take a long and narrow rectangular strip of paper. Bring the ends of the strip together to make a loop. Give one end a 180-degree (that is, a half-way round) twist so that the top surface meets the bottom surface. Tape the ends together. You now have a Möbius strip (or band). Start at any point on the surface and run your finger along the surface, you will end up where you started. You can try the same with the edge. Your strip has only one side and one edge.

Cut the strip down the middle all along its length. Instead of splitting into two strips, it turns into a single large strip with two half twists. It's no longer a Möbius strip. This unique property prompted some unknown wit to write the following limerick.

> *A mathematician confided*
> *That a Möbius strip is one sided,*
> *And you'll get quite a laugh*
> *If you cut it in half,*
> *For it stays in one piece when divided.*

Möbius was a mathematician and astronomer. His diaries reveal that he discovered his famous strip in 1858, but the discovery was published in 1865. After 150 years, the Möbius strip lives on beyond mathematics – in magic, art, literature, music, science and engineering (many conveyor and machinery belts are based on it to provide equal wear and tear on both sides).

Darwin's revolution

Charles Darwin (1809–82)

1859
England

Darwin's book presented his theory of evolution, which drastically modified our world view.

Evolution is the idea that all present-day species evolved from a single common ancestor through natural selection. All species tend to produce more offspring than can possibly survive, and the environment cannot support them all. Consequently, there's a struggle for existence. The individuals in all species vary among themselves and some individuals are better adapted for survival than others. This is the concept of 'survival of the fittest'. The offspring of the survivors inherit the favourable characteristics of their parents. This natural selection through time produces evolutionary change. 'Natural selection is an immensely powerful yet beautifully simple theory that has held up remarkably well, under intense and unrelenting scrutiny and testing' for nearly 150 years, says the world-renowned palaeontologist and author Stephen Jay Gould.

The first edition of *On the Origin of Species* sold out on the day of publication. Everyone was asking for a copy. The bewildered booksellers never dreamed that there would be such a demand for a biology tome. The book immediately polarised the society: it was highly praised by the many who believed in the new doctrine; it was loudly denounced by others for presenting an 'utterly rotten fabric of guess and speculation'. It still has the same polarising effect today.

On the Origin of Species – one of the most significant books ever written – ends with the words: 'There is grandeur in this view of life … from so simple a beginning endless forms most beautiful and most wonderful have been, and are being, evolved.'

1859
Germany

The greatest unsolved problem in mathematics

Bernhard Riemann (1826–66)

The Riemann hypothesis is a highly complex problem about the apparently random distribution of prime numbers.

Prime numbers are whole numbers (other than 1) that are divisible only by themselves and 1. The list starts with 2, 3, 5, 7, 11, 13, 17, 19, 23 … and continues indefinitely. By using computers, mathematicians today have uncovered the first 1.5 billion prime numbers. The list doesn't follow any regular pattern; the numbers appear to be distributed at random. But the solution of the Riemann hypothesis would reveal the mystery of the apparently random pattern of prime numbers.

Riemann, when he was 32 years old, presented a paper, 'On the Number of Prime Numbers Less Than a Given Quantity', to the Berlin Academy. In this paper he made a guess about the solution and then remarked: 'One would, of course, like to have a rigorous proof of this, but I have put aside the search for such a proof after some fleeting vain attempts.' The proof has tantalised almost all great mathematicians for 150 years. G.H. Hardy, a prominent English mathematician of the past century, had six ambitions in life. The first two were to prove the Riemann hypothesis, and to make 211 not out in a test match at the Oval cricket ground in London. He didn't achieve either of these!

Some mathematicians predict that the cracking of the Riemann hypothesis could result in financial disaster. Prime numbers are the key to cryptic codes, which keep internet commerce secure.

Tan's trouble

Pierre Broca (1824–80)

1861
France

Aphasia is a peculiar form of language disorder as a result of brain damage.

Broca was a neurologist working in Paris when a 21-year-old Monsieur Leborgne was admitted to his hospital. The unfortunate young man was affected by epilepsy and had lost the ability to speak. He understood speech perfectly well, but could only say 'tan' whenever asked a question. For this reason, he was nicknamed Tan. He died a few days later. When Broca performed an autopsy, he discovered a lesion in the left side of Tan's brain. He concluded that Tan's speech disorder was due to a lesion of the left hemisphere. After further research he named this speech disorder *aphémie* (which was later renamed aphasia).

Within a decade Karl Wernicke, a German neurologist, identified a second area of the brain, near the area identified by Broca, where damage causes another kind of speech disorder. Such patients can speak fluently, but what they say is meaningless; they can't understand speech and therefore they're unaware that they're talking nonsense. These two different kinds of language disorders are named after their discoverers: Broca's aphasia and Wernicke's aphasia. And if you suffer from 'whatsisname' condition (meaning you forget the names of people), it's called onomastic aphasia.

Broca once complained in a letter that 'private practice and marriage' were the twin extinguishers of science', yet his scientific work started the search for what areas of the brain did what. Locating the precise brain activity that creates specific behaviour responses is now an advanced science. A far cry from the head maps of phrenology (see p. 54).

'Let's learn to dream'

Friedrich Kekulé (1829–96)

Benzene is a ring-shaped molecule.

In 1854 the German chemist Kekulé was struggling with the idea of the structure of ethane, which contains two carbon and six hydrogen atoms. One night, while he was travelling by bus in London, he dreamed that: 'The atoms were gambolling before my eyes ... I saw frequently two smaller atoms united to form a pair; how a larger one embraced two smaller ones; how still larger ones kept hold of three or even four of the smaller; while the whole kept whirling in a giddy dance, I saw how the larger ones formed a chain, dragging the smaller ones after them but only at the ends of the chain.' The dream gave him the idea that the carbon atom can combine with four atoms, and that it's able to link in chains.

Kekulé knew that benzene contains six carbon and six hydrogen atoms, but he couldn't work out how the six carbons were arranged in space. Once again the solution came to him in a dream in 1865 when he was in Belgium: 'I turned my chair to the fire and dozed. Again the atoms were gambolling before my eyes. I could distinguish long rows of them twisting and twining in snakelike motion. Then one of the snakes grabbed hold of its own tail and began rotating before my eyes.' On awakening he saw the possibility that the six carbons could form a hexagonal ring. Kekulé, who once said 'let's learn to dream, then perhaps we will find the truth', laid the foundation of structural chemistry with his own dreams.

In 1850, when he was an architecture student, Kekulé attended the murder trial of a neighbour whose charred body had been found in her room. The famous chemist Justus von Liebig testified at the trial proving that the lady had died of spontaneous combustion because of drinking too much alcohol. The trial left a mark on Kekulé. He gave up architecture and took up the study of chemistry with Liebig.

'Where are these little beasts?'

1865
England

Joseph Lister (1827–1912)

Lister introduced the use of phenol as a disinfectant in surgery.

The discovery of anaesthetics (see p. 66) had done away with the agonised screams of patients, and yet still they often died of subsequent infections. When Lister, a surgeon, learned about Louis Pasteur's theory that germs are the cause of infections, he realised that infections in patients' wounds were caused by germs from the air and the surgeon's hands and instruments. He began searching for a substance that would protect wounds from germs. At that time phenol (also known as carbolic acid) was widely used in sewage farms to reduce odour, and Lister thought that it could be an effective disinfectant.

His first trial was on an eleven-year-old boy with a compound fracture. He used lint, soaked in phenol and linseed oil, as a dressing and left it in place for four days. The boy recovered completely. Lister further developed his method, which included changing the dressings regularly and spraying phenol in the air while the wound was exposed. In 1867 he published his results in the medical journal *Lancet*. But the medical profession was slow to recognise the value of his work. 'Where are these little beasts?' a prominent surgeon retorted when told of Lister's method. 'Show them to us and we shall believe in them. Has anyone seen them yet?'

The use of rubber gloves was introduced in 1894 by an American surgeon to protect the sensitive hands of his theatre-nurse fiancée against phenol. Lister's method became outdated by 1900 when operating theatres started sterilising everything.

The heat death of the universe

Rudolf Clausius (1822–88)

Entropy is a measure of disorder or randomness of a system.

Clausius, a theoretical physicist, was one of the founders of thermodynamics, the study of work, heat and other forms of energy. He developed thermodynamics from two laws. The first law of thermodynamics is the law of conservation of energy: energy is neither created nor destroyed. The second law, which he formulated himself, is the law of dissipation of energy: heat does not flow spontaneously from a colder to a hotter body (see p. 102 for the third law). Like Newton's laws, the second law is a scientific attempt to explain the universe. The law gives a direction to time – basically, it says that many natural processes are irreversible. One consequence of this irreversibility is the 'arrow of time'. Now you know why scrambled eggs can't be unscrambled.

In 1865 Clausius introduced the term entropy as a measure of disorder or randomness of a system. The more random or disordered a system is, the greater the entropy. In a closed system, entropy must ultimately reach a maximum. Entropy is continually increasing in the universe. But because the universe is a closed system, once all the energy in the universe is converted into heat, there will be no energy available for work. This would bring 'the heat death of the universe'.

This idea prompted the American novelist and poet John Updike to protest against entropy in his 'Ode to Entropy'.

> *Entropy!*
> *thou seal on extinction,*
> *thou curse on Creation.*
> *All change distributes energy,*
> *Spills what cannot be gathered again.*

Works like a dream

Dmitri Mendeleev (1834–1907)

1869
Russia

The periodic table is the greatest breakthrough in the history of chemistry.

Mendeleev, a professor of chemistry at the University of St Petersburg, was struggling with the problem of the order in which to introduce the 61 elements then known in his new textbook of chemistry. He listed the names and properties of the elements on individual cards and began a lengthy game of solitaire (patience), trying to arrange the cards in different ways. Tired, he fell asleep at his desk and dreamed. 'I saw in a dream a table', he wrote later, 'where all the elements fell into place as required.'

When he arranged the elements in order of their increasing atomic weights, he found that their properties repeated themselves periodically after each seven elements. He had discovered what we now call the periodic law, that the properties of the elements were the periodic functions of their atomic weights. So sure was he of his periodic law that he left gaps for three unknown elements and predicted their properties based on their positions in his table. Within twenty years, all three – gallium, scandium and germanium – had been found, and their properties matched his predictions.

In 1913 the English physicist Henry Moseley showed that the position of an element in the periodic table isn't governed by its atomic weight but by its atomic number (see p. 117). By 1925 chemists had successfully identified all the elements then believed to exist in nature. Mendeleev's name is enshrined in element 101, mendelevium, a transuranium element (see p. 140).

1872
England

Something is in the air

Robert Angus Smith (1817–84)

Acid rain contains enough acid to damage the environment.

In December 1952 a dark cloud of deadly smog – fog mixed with smoke from domestic fireplaces and power stations – enveloped London for four days, killing about 4,000 people. The effect of this smog was felt far beyond London. The wind carried the cloud for hundreds of miles before it fell as acid rain, killing aquatic life by increasing the acidity of lakes and rivers, damaging trees and corroding buildings.

The term 'acid rain' was first used by Smith, a Scottish chemist working in Manchester. He was one of the first chemists to study the chemistry of air pollution. In his book, *Air and Rain* (1872), he pointed out that acid rain was not only filthy but it attacked vegetation, stone and iron.

Normal rain is itself acidic – it reacts with carbon dioxide in the air to form weak carbonic acid with a pH of about 5.7. If the pH of rain or snow is lower than 5 – that is, more acidic than normal – it's called acid rain. One of the main causes of acid rain is sulphur dioxide, the gas produced by burning coal with high sulphur content. This was the gas that turned the London air into thick and yellowish 'pea soup' smog. Sulphur dioxide is converted into sulphuric acid in clouds by a series of chemical reactions. Another source of acid rain is the nitrogen dioxide given off by power stations and car exhausts, which is converted into nitric acid.

Don't answer that phone!

Alexander Graham Bell (1847–1922)

1876
USA

William Preece, chief engineer of the British Post Office at the time, remarked: 'Americans have need of the telephone, but we do not. We have plenty of messenger boys.'

Did you know the first words spoken on the telephone? 'Mr Watson, please come here, I want you.' Bell, a professor of vocal physiology at Boston University, tried out his new instrument for the first time through a transmitter set up in the attic of his house, and a receiver on the ground floor. A minute or two later, Thomas Watson, his assistant, stood before him, panting from running up the stairs. 'I could hear you!' he cried, 'It works!'

And it has been working ever since … and messenger boys were quickly dispensed with.

So why is it that we have such an overwhelming urge to answer the phone, even in the middle of more pressing business? The story goes that, in the 1910s, bean counters at Bell Telephone Company realised that if people answered their phones a little faster, Bell operators would be more productive and the savings, multiplied by company's vast number of telephone exchanges, would be substantial. The company launched an advertising campaign urging people to answer the phone more quickly. The person in charge of the campaign later boasted: 'I have made the Americans the only people in the world who will interrupt sex to answer the telephone.'

1879
France

Charming tales about little beasts

Jean Henri Fabre (1823–1915)

Souvenirs Entomologiques is the most fascinating collection of work on insects ever produced.

'Whenever reason has dominion, there dwells a severe beauty, a beauty which is the same in all the worlds and under all the stars. This universal beauty is order', writes Fabre, the celebrated entomologist and writer, in his lifetime work, *Souvenirs Entomologiques*, a collection of beautiful essays and illustrations on insects. Ten volumes of this colossal work were published from 1879 to 1907. Fabre devoted his entire life to the study of the anatomy and behaviour of insects. He wrote simply of what he saw in the gardens and fields near his home. His accounts, interspersed with many intimate biographical details, are almost like fairy tales and make delightful reading.

Born to a poverty-stricken family, he completed his university degree with the help of scholarships and became a teacher in the secondary school at Avignon. But his lifelong interest was in the natural history of insects. He had two trees opposite his house, under which he would sit all day long to observe the spider, fly, bee, grasshopper, wasp and other insects. The scientific precision of his observations led Charles Darwin to describe him as 'that inimitable observer', while the poetic beauty of his descriptions inspired Victor Hugo to call him 'the Homer of insects'. He is now remembered as the 'Insect Man'.

Entomologiques and Fabre's other works not only popularised entomology but set up the standards of observational patience and accuracy that future entomologists would have to match.

Sweet accidents

Constantine Fahlberg (1850–1910)

1879
USA

Saccharine was the first artificial sweetener discovered.

Fahlberg was a research assistant in the laboratory of the organic chemist Ira Remesen at John Hopkins University. One day he accidentally spilled some compound on his hands but didn't wash his hands thoroughly. Later that evening at dinner he noticed a sweet taste on his hands. He dubbed the substance 'saccharine' (after the Latin *saccharum*, meaning 'sugar') and took out a patent on it, which made him extremely wealthy. Remesen never forgave Fahlberg, calling him 'a scoundrel' for not acknowledging his contribution in synthesising the compound.

Saccharine is 300 times sweeter than sugar. Sweetness is a sensation in taste cells within taste buds which are situated on the tongue and soft palate. Saccharine has no calories as it's not digested by the body.

Two other popular sweeteners – cyclamate and aspartame – were also discovered accidentally. In 1937 Michael Sveda, a University of Illinois graduate student, was working on a compound called cyclamate. He left a cigarette on the laboratory bench for a moment and experienced a sensation of sweetness when he put the butt back in his mouth. Similarly, in 1965, a G.D. Searle pharmaceutical chemist James Schlatter was working on a cure for gastric ulcers when he licked his finger to pick up a piece of paper. He noticed a very strong, sweet taste, which he traced to aspartame (a popular sweetener nowadays). Nowadays smoking is banned in laboratories and wearing gloves is compulsory, making the chances of accidentally discovering another sweetener rather slim.

1882
Italy
1897
Germany

On the defence

Ilya Mechnikov (Russia, 1845–1916) and Paul Ehrlich (Germany, 1854–1915)

Immunity is the body's ability to fight the seemingly endless onslaught of viruses, bacteria and other invaders.

To fight these intruders, the body produces antibodies, specialised protein molecules that specifically bind to their target antigens. An antigen is a foreign molecule from a virus, bacterium or other invader. The invaders are opposed by scavenger cells, white blood cells called phagocytes, which simply engulf and digest the microbes. After engulfing the invader, some phagocytes called macrophages alert the rest of the immune system by displaying specific antigens on their surface. White blood cells called T lymphocytes recognise the antigen and send chemical signals to mobilise B lymphocytes, which secrete specific antibodies to neutralise the antigen. Some B and T cells form memory cells that circulate in the body for years, sometimes for a lifetime. This becomes the first line of defence against future infections.

Mechnikov and Ehrlich were the pioneers of immune system research. They shared the 1908 Nobel Prize for Physiology or Medicine in recognition of their work on immunity. Mechnikov, while working in Italy, noticed that when he inserted a thorn into a larva, strange cells gathered around the thorn. The cells started eating any foreign substances entering the ruptured skin. He named these new cells phagocytes ('cell eaters').

Ehrlich developed the key concept of antibodies, the molecules that simply destroy antigens by engulfing them. Ehrlich loved to explain his theories with diagrams and formulae. Sometimes he would become so excited that he would write on virtually any available surface – walls, doors, tablecloths, even his own shirt cuffs.

The lowest passing grade

Svante Arrhenius (1859–1927)

1884
Sweden

In ionic, or electrolytic, dissociation an ionic compound produces ions, charged atoms or molecules.

When an ionic compound such as sodium chloride is dissolved into water, it separates into positively charged sodium and negatively charged chloride ions. Once the ions are dissociated, an electric current can pass through the solution and the solution is called an electrolyte. Ionic dissociation has practical applications in industrial processes such electroplating.

Arrhenius was 22 when he became interested in the electrical conductivity of solutions. He decided to continue this work in preparation for his doctorate. For two years he performed hundreds of experiments on different solutions. But still he couldn't work out a theory to explain the results of his experiments. However, one night, the idea which was to give a new dimension to chemistry flashed through his mind. 'I got the idea in the night of 17th May, and I could not sleep that night until I had worked through the whole problem', he wrote later.

The examining committee found his doctoral thesis too novel, and awarded it the lowest passing grade. Even Per Teodor Cleve, his professor of chemistry, ignored it. 'If sodium chloride is dissolved into sodium and chlorine, why does not a solution of sodium chloride show properties of the elements sodium and chloride?' he asked. The discovery of the electron in 1890s proved once and for all that Arrhenius was right. In 1903 he was awarded the Nobel Prize for Chemistry for his theory.

See also GLOBAL WARMING, p. 93.

Kitchen sink chemistry

Agnes Pockels (1862–1935)

1891
Germany

Molecules at the surface of a liquid experience a force that makes the surface act like an elastic film, which tends to shrink to the smallest possible area.

They went to sea in a sieve, they did,
In a sieve they went to sea …

Pockels probably never read Edward Lear's *Nonsense Songs* (1871), but her pioneering experiments on the surface tension properties of water helped us to understand the wonderful 'skin' of water. She never had the opportunity to study science at school, yet she spent a lot of time at her kitchen sink observing the properties of oil and soap on the surface of water. When she heard of the English physicist Lord Rayleigh's experiments on surface tension, she wrote him a letter describing her first experiment. Lord Rayleigh translated the letter and sent it to the journal *Nature*, which published it in 1891.

Encouraged, she continued her research for the next 40 years and published fifteen other papers. On her 70th birthday, the chemist Wolfgang Ostwald paid tribute to her work: 'She taught us not only cleanliness in our work, she also taught us how to measure it.'

Let's drink a toast to this remarkable woman. Fill a wineglass with water up to the brim. Slide a paperclip carefully into the glass. Slide one more clip, and one more, and another … You'll need a large supply of paperclips to test the amazing 'skin' of water. Lear's song may not be complete nonsense after all.

Communicating with 10,000 neighbours

Santiago Ramón y Cajal (1852–1934)

Neurons, the nerve cells, are the building blocks of the nervous system.

In 1873 the Italian histologist Camillo Golgi developed a new staining technique in which he used silver salts to darken nerve tissues (histologists study the tissues of the body). The stained tissues revealed fine cellular components that are still called Golgi bodies. In 1887 Cajal, also a histologist, saw some nerve cells stained by the Golgi technique. He was mesmerised by the details. The nerve cells appeared 'coloured brownish black even to their finest branchlets, standing out with unsurpassable clarity upon a transparent yellow background. All was sharp as a sketch with Chinese ink', Cajal wrote in his memoirs.

Cajal modified Golgi's technique and applied it to brain tissues. At that time it was believed that the nervous system was a network of continuous elements, but Cajal found that the branches, or axons, of the nerve cells terminate near other nerve cells. This suggested that the nervous system was made up of billions of separate nerve cells which worked by contact. In 1891 the German anatomist Wilhelm Waldeyer coined the term 'neuron' and Cajal's ideas became known as the neuron theory. Cajal shared the 1906 Nobel Prize for Physiology or Medicine with Golgi.

We know now that neurons carry an electrical signal from one to another. Each neuron connects with up to 10,000 neighbours. Cajal's ideas led to the understanding of synapses (the tiny gap between axons, which are the sites of neuron-to-neuron communication), and have had a great impact on medicine.

Alive or dead?

Dmitri Ivanovski (1864–1920)

Although viruses posses some characteristics of living things, they lack many features essential for life.

Like living cells, viruses have proteins and the genetic materials DNA and RNA, but they can replicate only when inside the living cell of an organism. Once inside a cell, viruses exploit the cell's machinery to manufacture more viruses. Most viruses range in size from twenty to 300 nanometres.

The story of the discovery of viruses is linked with the tobacco mosaic disease, which is so named because of the dark and light spots it causes on the leaves of tobacco plants. Ivanovski, a botanist, suggested that the disease was either caused by a toxin (the word virus comes from the Latin word for poison) or by a life form far smaller than any other that's known. It was only in 1935 that viruses were demoted to inert chemicals when the American scientist Wendell Stanley crystallised the tobacco mosaic virus.

The human immunodeficiency virus (HIV), which causes AIDS, is a retrovirus. In a retrovirus, the genetic information is in the form of a single strand of RNA. It makes DNA when inside a host cell. The viral DNA then joins the host cell's DNA and becomes part of the host's genetic information code. The evolutionary history of viruses is as old as the history of life. However, the HIV virus has a very short evolutionary history (probably starting from 1959), and it's been the only evolutionary history of an organism witnessed by scientists.

Chemistry thrown with a shovel

1894
Germany

Friedrich Wilheim Ostwald (1853–1932)

A catalyst is a substance that can either speed up or slow down a chemical reaction, but is not itself changed in the reaction.

Ostwald's concept of catalysts still holds true. It's extremely useful in many modern technological processes such as the Haber process (see p. 108) and the catalytic converters in automobile exhaust systems. Platinum and palladium are used in exhaust systems as catalysts to convert carbon monoxide, nitrogen oxides and other harmful fumes into environmentally friendly gases.

The Swedish chemist Jöns Berzelius (see p. 61) was first to use the word catalyst, but Ostwald gave it its modern meaning when he first proved the catalytic action of enzymes. Living cells produce proteins called enzymes, which act as catalysts for all chemical reactions that take place in living cells. For example, an enzyme called amylase in our saliva increases the rate at which starch is converted into sugars.

Ostwald, who is one of the founders of physical chemistry, was awarded the 1909 Nobel Prize for Chemistry. 'It has pleased no less than surprised me that of the many studies whereby I have sought to extend the field of general chemistry, the highest scientific distinction that there is today has been awarded for those on *catalysis*', he noted in his Nobel lecture. He taught for a while at the University of Riga in Latvia where his lectures aroused much interest. 'He sees to it that chemistry goes into your head as though thrown with a shovel', a student once commented. Peculiarly, the popular professor was phobic about being touched by strangers such as barbers and tailors.

1895
Germany

'These naughty, naughty Röntgen rays'

Wilhelm Röntgen (1845–1923)

X-rays are the invisible electromagnetic radiation of very short wavelengths.

One evening Röntgen was experimenting with a Crookes tube in his darkened laboratory. When electricity is discharged through the tube its walls become phosphorescent. By chance he happened to note that a paper lying on his work table glowed brightly when he passed the current through the tube. The paper was coated in a florescent solution and at first he thought it was merely a reflection from the electric spark. But it puzzled him as the tube was thoroughly covered with a shield of black cardboard – until he realised that some unknown radiation was passing through it.

Then he had the brilliant idea that this radiation might also affect photographic plates. He persuaded his wife to place her hand between the glass tube and a photographic plate. When he developed the plate he saw the shadow of the bones of her wife's hand. He named this new radiation an X-ray.

The possibility of photographing bones through flesh started extravagant and fanciful speculations at the turn of the century, before X-rays became a major medical diagnostic tool. An enterprising London firm made a small fortune from selling X-ray-proof underwear, while a newspaper claimed that no one would be interested in an X-ray portrait which would show 'only the bones and rings on the fingers'. The satirical magazine Punch also joined in the fun.

> *The fondest swain would scarcely prize*
> *A picture of his lady's framework;*
> *To gaze on this with yearning eyes*
> *Would probably be voted tame work.*

On the therapist's couch

Sigmund Freud (1856–1939)

1896
Austria

Freudian psychoanalysis is based on the belief that our emotions and behaviour arise from unconscious fears and desires.

You may have never read a word of Freud's major works – *The Interpretation of Dreams* (1900) and *Three Essays on the Theory of Sexuality* (1905) – but you probably know some Freud speak: Oedipus complex, id, ego, superego, sexual sublimation, repressed memories, and so on. And you can't say that you have never made a Freudian slip (an unintentional error in speech that Freud would have explained as a message from your unconscious mind revealing your suppressed thoughts or feelings).

According to psychoanalysis, the past shapes the present, and if we can trace the source of our unconscious fears and desires to their historical origins – often our childhood experiences – we can understand our troubles and deal better with the realities of life. All you have to do is to lie on the therapist's couch and talk about anything that comes to mind – and the source of your current problems would slowly begin to appear.

Freud changed the way we see ourselves, but the question remains: is psychoanalysis an objective science or a scientific blunder? Psychoanalysis has not yet proved itself empirically a science; nor has psychoanalysis yet been proved quackery. 'If often he was wrong and, at times, absurd, to us he is no more a person now but a whole climate of opinion.' This comment from the poet W. H. Auden after Freud's death in 1939 still holds true, and the present climate of opinion is cloudy.

1896
France

On a cloudy day in Paris

Henri Becquerel (1852–1908)

Radioactivity is the spontaneous emission of radiation from unstable atoms.

Becquerel, an obscure physics professor in Paris, was interested in fluorescence and phosphorescence. A fluorescent substance glows under light and stops glowing as soon as light is turned off, but a phosphorescent substance continues to glow for a while. The discovery of X-rays made him wonder whether they were also emitted by phosphorescent substances when exposed to sunlight.

He placed some crystals of a salt of uranium on a photographic plate and wrapped them in thick black paper to keep the light out. He expected the crystals to produce X-rays when left in the sunlight. As the sun did not shine for several days, he left the packet in a dark drawer. After a few overcast days he decided to develop the plate nevertheless. To his surprise, he discovered a sharp image on it. He repeated his experiment on various salts of uranium and showed that the radiation was different from X-rays, although he didn't explain what caused the radiation.

Becquerel's chance discovery opened a new chapter in science. It attracted the attention of a young Polish-born scientist, Marie Curie. She chose Becquerel's newly discovered phenomenon as the topic for her doctorate, and named it radioactivity. She showed that uranium wasn't the only substance that emitted spontaneous radiation, which was due to changes within atoms. Later Pierre, her French-born physicist husband, also joined her and both discovered two new elements, polonium and radium. They shared the 1903 Nobel Prize for Physics with Becquerel.

The prediction of a 'retired brewer'

1896
Sweden

Svante Arrhenius (1859–1927)

Arrhenius was the first to recognise the greenhouse effect, the cause of global warming.

Water vapour, carbon dioxide, methane and nitrous oxide make up less than 1 per cent of Earth's atmosphere, but they play an important role in keeping our planet at a constant temperature. These natural gases – and some human-made gases such as chloro-fluorocarbons – allow the sunlight to enter freely, but absorb heat radiated from Earth's surface. Nature's blanket keeps Earth at an ideal temperature by balancing the amount of heat received from the Sun with the amount of heat lost from the surface.

Arrhenius (see p. 85) suggested that the burning of fossil fuels would increase carbon dioxide in the atmosphere, which would bring about significant changes to our climate – but Arrhenius's warning was ignored by the scientists of the day.

Even as a young man, Arrhenius was stockily built. After completing his doctorate in Sweden he went to Germany for further studies. One day he heard one of the German students remark: 'Here comes the brainy foreigner. I wonder if all Swedes look like retired brewers.'

It's time we heeded the brainy scientist who could pass as a brewer. The global temperature has risen by 0.6ºC since his warning, and is now rising at a rate of about 0.2ºC per decade. The amount of carbon dioxide in the atmosphere has risen by 34 per cent since 1750, and global carbon dioxide emissions continue to rise. About three-quarters of carbon dioxide emissions are from burning fossils fuels.

See also SCIENTIFIC EVIDENCE FOR CLIMATE CHANGE, p. 192.

1897
England

The jolly electron

Joseph John ('J.J.') Thomson (1856–1940)

The discovery of the electron, the first subatomic particle, destroyed the long-held view that atoms were the smallest particles.

Though Crookes at first suspected my presence on this earth
'Twas J. J. that found me – in spite of my tiny girth.
He measured first the 'e by m' of my electric worth:
I love J. J. in a filial way, for he it was gave me birth.

With this song, workers at the Cavendish Laboratory in Cambridge celebrated the Nobel Prize-winning physicist's 70th birthday. In 1879 the English physicist William Crookes performed an experiment using an evacuated glass tube with two metal electrodes sealed in opposite ends and connected to a high-voltage source. He noticed a stream of rays coming from the cathode, or negative electrode. He speculated that the cathode rays, as the rays were called, consisted of tiny particles. The Irish physicist George Stoney even suggested a name for these particles – electrons.

Thomson showed that cathode rays could be deflected by a magnetic or electric field. He concluded that cathode rays were streams of negatively charged particles; and these particles came from the atoms of the metal cathode. When he announced his results at the Royal Institution on 30 April 1897, many scientists refused to believe that there existed a particle lighter than the atom. Someone even suggested that Thomson was pulling their legs. Thomson later measured the ratio of charge e to the mass m of the electron, which was refined in 1909 by Millikan (see p. 110). In 1906, Thomson was awarded his Nobel Prize for Physics, for the discovery of the electron.

See also NUCLEAR MODEL OF THE ATOM, p. 111.

'A secret hidden since the world began'

1897
India

Ronald Ross (1857–1932)

Mosquitoes transmit malaria parasites.

Ross was a medical officer in the British army in India when he met Patrick Manson, the 'father of tropical medicine', on a visit to London in 1894. Manson had demonstrated in 1878 that parasites that cause human disease could infect mosquitoes. Ross was also familiar with the work of the French physician Charles Laveran who in 1880, while stationed in Algeria, had discovered that malaria was caused by a protozoan, a one-celled microscopic animal. However, he never found how the parasites entered the bloodstreams of humans. On his return to India in 1895, Ross was determined to solve the mystery of malaria, then the most common infectious disease throughout the tropics.

He was convinced that malaria was caused by mosquitoes, but the connection eluded him until 20 August 1897, when he peered through his microscope to examine the stomach tissue of a dapple-winged mosquito. It had been fed four days previously with the blood from a malaria patient and now Ross found 'something new … exactly like the pigment of the parasite of malaria'. After further research he conclusively proved that malaria was transmitted by the mosquito bite. He was awarded the 1902 Nobel Prize for Physiology or Medicine for this discovery.

Ross, who loved playing piano and writing poetry, would have appreciated this poem his friend the English poet John Masefield wrote on the 60th anniversary of the momentous discovery.

> *Once on the August day, an exiled man*
> *Striving to read hieroglyphics spelled*
> *By changing speckles on glass, beheld*
> *A secret hidden since the world began.*

'So they do exist'

Max Planck (1858–1947)

The photon is the basic unit, or quantum, of electromagnetic radiation.

While working on the problem of how the amount of heat given off by a body is related to its temperature, Planck came up with a formula that explained the experimental data. But the formula made sense only when he assumed that the energy of a vibrating molecule was quantised, that is, it could only take on certain values. At that time scientists believed that radiation must flow continuously. Planck's formula suggested that radiation flows in discrete packets (he called them quanta; and the singular, quantum) whose energy was proportional to the frequency of radiation. The relationship between energy (E) and frequency (f) required a constant to make it an equation, $E = hf$. The new universal constant, h, is called Planck's constant. (According to a Russian story, in an oral exam a professor wrote the equation $E = hf$ and asked a student: 'What is h?' 'Plank's constant', the student replied. 'And f?' 'The length of the plank.')

Planck was doubtful about the reality of his quanta, but in 1905 Einstein applied the concept in his theory of photoelectric effect. In 1926, the American chemist Gilbert Lewis coined the term 'photons' for quanta.

Planck's quantum idea gave birth to the new quantum physics. Planck was a theoretical physicist, not an experimental scientist. He once visited a physics laboratory where he saw in action an apparatus that counted light quanta, or photons, by audible clicks. He stood silently for a while and just listened. Then he smiled and murmured: 'So they do exist.'

The 'S' that changed the world

1901
England–
Canada

Guglielmo Marconi (1874–1937)

The first transatlantic wireless transmission on 12 December 1901 ushered in the era of worldwide electronic communication.

It was a cold, bitter day. Marconi and some of his assistants were huddled around a radio receiver in a wooden hut near St John's in Newfoundland. He put on his headphones, but heard only static. There was no signal from the radio transmitter he had set up at Podhu in Cromwell 3,440 kilometres away.

The young Italian inventor, who would win the 1909 Nobel Prize for Physics, had spent years planning for this day. 'An Italian has arrived – with a concertina but no monkey. It is a street organ which it is impossible to play, but it can make a lot of noise', a London newspaper commented in 1896 when Marconi arrived in England with his experimental apparatus for transmitting and receiving radio messages.

The first transatlantic telegraph cable had been laid in 1857; Marconi wanted to send messages without cables – by the wireless telegraph he'd invented. No one at the time knew whether radio waves followed the curvature of Earth or went straight into space. If they didn't follow the curvature, he would fail. 'Suddenly, about half past twelve there sounded three sharp little clicks of the "tapper", showing me that something was coming', Marconi recalled later. The radio waves had travelled around the world from England to Canada carrying three dots of the letter 'S' in the Morse code (dots and dashes representing letters and numbers). The world was forever changed.

1901
Sweden

'The most worthy shall receive the prize'

Alfred Nobel (1833–96)

In the sciences, prizes are awarded in physics, chemistry, physiology or medicine (and, since 1969, in economics).

After an explosion in the family's nitroglycerine factory killed his brother, Alfred Nobel, an industrialist and inventor, decided to tame this dangerously unstable liquid explosive. In 1866 he discovered that nitroglycerine, when mixed with a rare earth called kieselguhr, could be shaped into sticks safe to handle. He called his discovery 'dynamite', and made a fortune from it. A year before his death he wrote his last will, leaving his estate for the establishment of annual prizes in five fields: three in science, one in literature and one in peace. 'No consideration whatever shall be given to the nationality of the candidates, but that the most worthy shall receive the prize', he wrote.

The prizes have been awarded every year since 1901. The winners receive a gold medal bearing a replica of Nobel's profile and a cheque (in recent years it has been for more than US$1 million). Nobel once said: 'If you have a thousand ideas and only one turns out to be good, I am satisfied.' One of his good ideas has helped over 1,000 excellent ideas to flourish.

In Nobel Prize trivia: only four people have received two Nobel Prizes. Linus Pauling, from the USA, is the only person who has won twice without having shared the prize: for Chemistry (1954) and Peace (1962). Fellow American John Bardeen shared the Physics prize twice, in 1956 and 1972. Frederick Sanger, UK, won the prize for Chemistry on his own in 1958 and shared it in 1980. Marie Curie, from Poland, shared the 1903 Physics prize and won the 1911 Chemistry prize alone.

A barber's dilemma

Bertrand Russell (1872–1970)

1902
England

Is the set of all sets which are not members of themselves a member of itself?

A set is a collection of elements. These elements are called members. Sets either are or are not members themselves. Consider S, a set that contains members which are (a) sets; and (b) not members of themselves. Is S a member of S? If S is a member of S, then it fails to meet the requirement to *not* be a member of itself. But if S is not a member of S, then it meets the requirements to be a member of S. This is known as Russell's paradox.

In 1902 Russell, a philosopher and mathematician and the future Nobel Laureate in Literature (1950), presented this paradox in a letter to the German mathematician Gottlob Frege. To explain the paradox to non-mathematicians, Russell proposed in 1918 the 'barber paradox'. A village barber has the following sign on his shop: 'I shave only and all men in the village who do not shave themselves'. Does the barber shave himself? If he does shave himself, he would belong to the set of men who shave themselves – meaning he shouldn't shave himself. If he doesn't shave himself and decides to wear a full beard, then he *should* do so according to the sign. This is the barber's predicament, at least, until he takes the sign down.

Russell also famously remarked that the Ten Commandments should be headed (like an examination paper): 'Not more than six to be attempted.'

See also CATCH-22 PARADOX, p. 159.

1903
France

The rays of delusion

René Blondlot (1849–1930)

N-rays are one of the biggest blunders in the history of science.

Blondlot, a highly respected physicist at the University of Nancy, was experimenting with newly discovered X-rays when he noticed some strange things about the radiation coming out of his apparatus. He thought he had discovered a new kind of radiation and named it N-rays after his university. He claimed mysterious properties for N-rays, such as they could be stored in various things, a brick for example, and if you held the brick close to your head, the rays would increase your ability to see in the dark.

Many scientists were sceptical of these claims. In 1904, when American physicist Robert Wood learned about the N-rays, he decided to pay Blondlot a visit. Blondlot showed him the apparatus in his darkened laboratory and read various measurements loudly. Wood quietly put an aluminium prism, which was a crucial part of the apparatus, in his pocket and asked Blondlot to repeat the measurements. The new measurements were perfectly similar to the earlier ones. Wood published his report in the prestigious journal *Nature* claiming that N-rays were nothing but a delusion. 'What a spectacle for French science when one of its distinguished savants measures the positions of the spectrum line, while the prism reposes in the pocket of his American colleague!' exclaimed a French scientist.

Wood's report ended one of the biggest blunders in the history of science. Was it a case of self-delusion or a conscious effort to perpetrate a hoax? We simply don't know.

Without needles or incisions

1903
Holland

Wilhelm Einthoven (1860–1927)

The electrocardiogram measures and records the electrical activity of the heart.

After Galvani's experiments with frogs (see p. 51) scientists knew that muscular contractions produce electric currents. In 1887 the French physiologist Augustus Waller reasoned that one could assess the functioning of the heart by measuring its electric current. The challenge was to measure these tiny currents with sufficient accuracy. He placed a series of small glass tubes filled with mercury on the surface of the body. Mercury rose and fell with the changes in the impulses from the heart. He projected the images of rising and falling mercury onto a photographic paper and called it a cardiograph. He failed to find any clinical applications for his device.

Einthoven, a professor of physiology at the University of Leyden and a good friend of Waller, started testing Waller's apparatus in his laboratory which was located in an old wooden building near a cobblestone street. Whenever heavy horse wagons would pass by, the building shook – making the readings of the cardiogram fluctuate.

The frustrated professor decided to design a precise and reliable instrument. He modified a galvanometer, a device for detecting small electric currents, by replacing its heavy coil of wire (suspended between the poles of a horseshoe magnet) with a thin silver-coated quartz string. As the string deflected in response to electric current, its delicate movements could be recorded on a paper. He called the instrument an electrocardiogram. He was honoured with the 1924 Nobel Prize for Physiology or Medicine for his invention, which proved an invaluable diagnostic tool in medicine.

1905
Germany

Cowshed thermodynamics

Walther Nernst (1864–1941)

It's impossible to cool a substance to a temperature of absolute zero (–273.15°C).

Simply put, absolute zero is unattainable. We can approach it as closely as we wish, but we can't actually achieve it. Entropy (see p. 78) explains this paradox. When the temperature of a substance approaches absolute zero, its entropy approaches zero. Steam, for example, has a higher entropy than liquid water, as its molecules have a higher kinetic energy and move faster. Its entropy decreases when it condenses into liquid, and decreases much more when it freezes into ice. Its entropy would be zero if we continued cooling it to absolute zero, and all molecular motion (which is what constitutes heat) would stop completely. Atoms and molecules can't be idle; that's against the laws of physics – so this process is impossible.

Nernst was one of the greats of German science and his most famous contributions were in thermodynamics and electro-chemistry. He was awarded the 1920 Nobel Prize for Chemistry for his discovery of the third law of thermodynamics.

One cold winter morning Nernst happened to visit the cowshed in his country estate. He found it pleasantly warm, though there was no heating equipment. When he enquired why the cowshed was so warm, he was told that the cows themselves gave off heat. The famous chemist quickly realised that the cows used a portion of their feed to keep themselves warm. He immediately decided to sell his cows and invest instead in raising fish, which are always in thermodynamic equilibrium with their surroundings, in the estate's ponds.

The elusive atoms

Albert Einstein (1879–1955)

1905
Switzerland

The idea of the atom has been around since the time of the ancient Greeks, but Einstein was the first to provide a mathematical proof for their existence.

If you look at the dust particles in a sunbeam, you notice that they're continuously moving. In fact, solid particles suspended in a fluid are in constant motion. This restless motion is called Brownian motion after Scottish botanist Robert Brown who discovered it in 1827 when he was using a microscope to view tiny pollen grains in water. Brown couldn't explain the cause of this motion.

Einstein's face – the wild-haired old man with piercing eyes – is now an icon of science but in 1905 he was only 26 years old, an anonymous clerk in the Swiss Patent Office in Berne. In that year he published three papers – all of them written in his spare time – that shook the world. The second paper was on Brownian motion. In this paper he showed mathematically that the motion of larger solid particles suspended in a fluid is caused by the movement of tiny molecules of the fluid. The molecules of a fluid are always vibrating and this motion causes them to continually collide with larger particles. He also calculated the mean free path of solid particles, the average distance a particle would travel between collisions.

Einstein's theoretical work proved the existence of molecules, and therefore the atoms they're made of. It spurred French physicist Jean Perrin to perform painstaking experiments on emulsions containing microscopic particles of gamboge pigment, proving in 1908 that atoms do exist.

See also SPECIAL RELATIVITY, p. 104.

1905
Switzerland

A new way of looking at time

Albert Einstein (1879–1955)

Time is not an absolute quantity. Our measurements of time are not affected by our motion.

Einstein's third paper in 1905 (see p. 103) became known as the theory of special relativity. The two fundamental assumptions of this theory are: (a) the laws of physics are the same in all frames of reference; and (b) the speed of light is constant and is independent of the speed of the observer.

These assumptions have two bizarre consequences. First, a moving clock runs slower than a stationary one with respect to a stationary observer. 'If you wanted to live longer, you could keep flying to the east so that the speed of plane is added to the earth's rotation', advises the British physicist Stephen Hawking. 'However, the tiny fraction of a second you gained would be more than offset by eating airline meals.' Second, a moving object appears to contract in the direction of motion, as seen by a stationary observer. The contraction is negligible unless the object's speed is close to the speed of light.

According to a story, probably apocryphal, Elsa, Einstein's second wife, once visited a high-tech laboratory in the United States. She was shown some huge, gleaming equipment and told that it was used for probing the deepest secrets of the universe. 'Is that all', replied Mrs Einstein. 'My husband did that on the back of old envelopes.' Well, we don't know whether the theory of special relativity was drafted on scraps of papers, but it certainly changed the way we look at time dramatically.

'Godnose' whether it's A, B, C, D, E or K

Frederick Hopkins (1861–1947)

Vitamins are organic molecules which are essential to the diet of humans.

At the beginning of the 19th century, scientists believed that a healthy diet consisted of a proper mixture of fats, proteins, carbohydrates, minerals and water. Hopkins, a biochemist, was interested in the study of diet and its effect on metabolism. In 1906 he noticed that his laboratory rats failed to grow when fed on a diet of pure fats, proteins and carbohydrates. But the rats grew rapidly when he added even a tiny amount of yeast extract to their diet. He concluded that 'no animal can live upon a mixture of pure protein, fat, and carbohydrate'. He suggested that diseases such as rickets and scurvy were caused by this missing dietary substance. Hopkins continued his research and later identified two mysterious components which became known as vitamins A and D. The thirteen known vitamins in the human diet are named by letters: A, the eight B vitamins (originally thought to be one vitamin), C, D, E and K.)

In 1912 the Polish biochemist Casimir Funk coined the term 'vitamine' when he discovered the vitamin niacin (B3). When Hungarian biochemist Albert Szent-Györgyi submitted his paper announcing the discovery of vitamin C to the journal *Nature* he named it 'ignose' as it was a sugar of unknown composition. The editor considered the term too flippant and rejected it. Szent-Györgyi sent back his paper with the compound renamed 'godnose'.

Hopkins's discovery, for which he was awarded the 1929 Nobel Prize for Physiology or Medicine, laid the groundwork for the study of vitamins.

1907
USA

Our future in plastics

Leo Baekeland (1863–1944)

**Bakelite was the first synthetic plastic. Forgive the cliché,
it did change the world.**

In 1893 Baekeland, a Belgian-born chemist, invented a photo-graphic paper, Velox, which could be developed by artificial light. Earlier papers had to be printed in sunlight. Velox attracted the attention of George Eastman, who introduced the Kodak camera and the slogan 'you press the button, we do the rest' to the world. At the meeting to discuss the deal to buy Velox, Eastman immedi-ately offered Baekeland US$1 million (an amazing sum in those days). Baekeland had decided to ask for $50,000 and would have gone as low as $25,000 if Eastman didn't agree. 'I was fortunate that I was seated; otherwise I would have gone through the roof', he recalled later.

Suddenly a millionaire at 35, Baekeland was now ready for his next big invention. He knew that the booming electrical industry was looking for an alternative insulator for wires. The demand for the common insulator shellac, a natural resinous material, was out-stripping supply. After three years of experiments, Baekeland again hit the jackpot. He'd made a hard translucent substance – and dubbed it Bakelite – from phenol and formaldehyde which could be moulded easily into any shape. Bakelite, the first true plastic, soon became the material for making everything, from car engine parts to artificial jewellery.

If you have seen the movie *The Graduate* (1967), you may recall Mr McGuire saying: 'I just want to say one word to you. Just one word: plastic. There's a great future in plastics.' Baekeland invented that future.

Bread and butterfly effects

Jules-Henri Poincaré (1854–1912)

1908
France

The behaviour of a dynamic system depends on its small initial conditions.

'Small differences in the initial conditions produce very great ones in the final phenomena. A small error in the former will produce an enormous error in the latter. Prediction becomes impossible.' Poincaré, the renowned mathematician and philosopher of science, made this observation in his book, *Science and Method* (1908).

Poincaré's observation received little attention from his contemporaries, but earned him the title of the 'founder of chaos theory'. The first study of chaotic behaviour in nature was made by the American meteorologist Edward Lorenz in 1963, when he developed a computer model to predict weather patterns. He was surprised to find that even a small change in initial values resulted in wildly different conditions in his predictions. This is sometimes called the 'butterfly effect': an action as small as a butterfly flapping its wings, say in Sydney, could bring about a snowstorm weeks later thousands of kilometres away in London. Chaotic behaviour occurs in phenomena as diverse as the stock market, population changes and the human heartbeat.

There's also an absolutely non-chaotic story, probably apocryphal, about Poincaré, who was in the habit of buying fresh bread every day from his local baker. He suspected that the bread weighed less than the advertised weight of one kilogram. He started weighing the bread daily at his home. After a year, he plotted the graph of daily weights, which showed a bell-curve with the minimum weight of 950 grams but truncated on the left side of the kilogram mark. He reported the matter to the authorities.

1908
Germany

The fertiliser revolution

Fritz Haber (1868–1934)

In the Haber process, nitrogen from the air is extracted to produce ammonia.

In the early 19th century the most widely used artificial fertiliser in Europe was potassium nitrate which came from islands off Chile and Peru. Before the First World War, the Allied blockade cut off Germany's supply of this essential farming commodity. German chemists started looking for other ways of making nitrogen compounds, as nitrogen is essential for plant growth. Nitrogen makes up about four-fifths of the atmosphere, but no one had ever discovered a way of 'fixing' it into a compound. Haber's ingenious solution was to pass a mixture of nitrogen and hydrogen over iron, which serves as a catalyst, at a very high pressure and temperature. The gases combine to form ammonia which is then used to make nitrate fertilisers.

Haber was fond of telling a story. After a long walk on a hot day he arrived at a water trough in a village. He buried his face in the cold water. Unknown to him an ox had also dipped his head into the water on the other side of the trough. When they raised their head, they stared each other and discovered that they had exchanged heads. Haber would finish his creepy tale: 'And since that time …'

Since that time, at least, the Haber process has made nitrate fertilisers cheap. It could be said that this process is the most important chemical reaction in history. It has contributed to sustaining massive growth in the human population over the past century.

Unravelling Earth's layers

Andrija Mohorovičić (1857–1936)

1900
Croatia

The boundary between Earth's crust and mantle is called the Moho.

In the 1900s geologists were certain that Earth was made of many layers, like an onion, but they weren't sure where the layers started and stopped. The seismograph – an instrument for recording the shock waves that travel in all directions after an earthquake – was also developed around the same time. Mohorovičić, one of the first seismologists, helped establish a network of seismic recording stations in Croatia. When an earthquake shook the Kupa Valley in 1909, he was well equipped to make a scientific study of this geological event.

The recordings of the Croatian stations clearly showed two kinds of seismic waves. Stations nearer to the earthquake recorded slow-travelling waves, but the recordings from more distant stations showed fast-travelling waves. He interpreted that the slow waves travelled directly from the centre of the earthquake through the crust, while the fast waves must have passed through a layer of denser rocks below the crust (waves speed up when they pass through denser rocks). He concluded that there was a layer of separation – a discontinuity – between the crust and the mantle.

Geologists have now traced the Moho (short for Mohorovičić discontinuity) worldwide. It exists at an average depth of eight kilometres beneath the ocean basins and about 32 kilometres beneath the continents. They've also discovered two other boundaries: one between the mantle and the core, and the other between the liquid outer core and the solid inner core.

'All I saw was a wink'

Robert Millikan (1868–1953)

Millikan's famous oil-drop experiment showed that the electron is the fundamental unit of electricity.

Millikan's apparatus simply consisted of a small box attached to a microscope. Surrounding the box were two brass plates. An atomiser introduced oil drops between the plates. By adjusting the voltage the charge on the plates could be changed until the drops were in mid-air. At this moment, the charge on the drop (upward electric force) equalled its weight (downward force of gravity). From this data Millikan calculated the absolute charge on the electron, which is by convention called unit negative, –1, charge.

In recent years, the Nobel laureate Millikan has come under criticism for 'cooking' his experimental data. Cooking data means using only those results that fit the theory and discarding others. His laboratory notebooks do reveal he was selective in using his data. The American poet Robert Frost was on the ball in 'A Wish to Comply', published in 1949 long before the current controversy:

> Did I see it go by,
> That Millikan mote?
> Well, I said that I did.
> I made a good try.
> But I'm no one to quote.
> If I have a defect
> It's a wish to comply
> And see as I'm bid.
> I rather suspect
> All I saw was the lid
> Going over my eye.
> I honestly think
> All I saw was a wink.

An icon of science

Ernest Rutherford (1871–1937)

1911
England

Rutherford's picture of the atom – speeding electrons orbiting a tiny Sun-like nucleus – is familiar to everyone.

The first real picture of the internal structure of the atom emerged in 1897 when the British physicist J. J. Thomson suggested that the atom was like a Christmas pudding, in which negatively charged electron 'raisins' are embedded in a spherical 'pudding' of positively charged protons. This delicious model was soon replaced by a superior model advanced by his student. Rutherford's model showed that the atom contained a dense nucleus composed of positively charged protons and neutral neutrons. Most of the atom was empty space – with the electrons, like the planets round the Sun, moving about the tiny central nucleus.

This model soon became an icon by which we still recognise the atom. Though it's essentially correct, it has a major drawback: according to classical physics a rotating electron must radiate energy and therefore describes a path of ever decreasing radius until it spirals into the nucleus. Rutherford's model has now been replaced by the quantum model of the atom (see p. 116).

New Zealand-born Rutherford, a physicist, was awarded the 1908 Nobel Prize for Chemistry for his work on radioactivity. He delighted in telling friends, the fastest transformation he knew of was his transformation from a physicist to a chemist. On his death the *New York Times* noted: 'It is given to but few men to achieve immortality, still less to achieve Olympian rank, during their own lifetime. Lord Rutherford achieved both.'

The path of no resistance

Heike Kamerlingh Onnes (1853–1926)

A superconductor carries electricity without any resistance.

An electric current is the flow of electrons through a conductor. As electrons hop from one atom to the next through a conductor, they lose a little energy in the form of heat. A superconductor carries electricity without any loss of energy. Kamerlingh Onnes, a physicist at the University of Leyden, dedicated his life to the study of materials at extremely low temperatures. Absolute zero (a temperature of −273.15°C) is the lowest theoretical limit of temperature. Atoms and molecules of all materials are always in motion, but at this temperature they'd stop vibrating. The laws of physics dictate that absolute zero can be approached as closely as we wish, but it can never actually be achieved.

In 1908 Kamerlingh Onnes managed to cool helium to −268°C. He was right when he declared that the coldest place on Earth was situated at Leyden. He immersed various metals in liquid helium in order to study their properties and was surprised to find that mercury completely lost its resistance at this low temperature. He published his results in 1911 and two years later '*le gentleman du zéro absolu*', as he was now known in his country, was awarded the Nobel Prize for Physics for his discovery.

The hottest superconductor so far built works at a temperature of −103°C. Room-temperature superconductivity is on the wish list of scientists. If achieved, it would open ways to many technical marvels, from superfast computer processors to eco-friendly trains and ships powered by electricity.

A cosmic hazard

Victor Hess (1833–1964)

1912
Austria

Cosmic rays are elementary particles that travel through the universe at nearly the speed of light.

For some time scientists had been puzzled by the fact that air in gold-leaf electroscopes became electrically charged no matter how well the instruments were sealed. (A gold-leaf electroscope is a simple device to measure electric charge. Two strips of gold leaf repel each other when charged, but when radiation ionises the air, the charge is leaked off and the strips slowly come together.) What was ionising the air then, allowing it to conduct electricity? Some scientists blamed the radioactivity of the soil, but Hess, a physicist at the Vienna Academy of Science, speculated that the source of radiation might be located in the air rather than on the ground. He undertook a series of balloon flights to test his hypothesis.

His flights showed that the ionisation in his hermetically sealed instruments noticeably increased from 1,000 metres upwards. To rule out the Sun as the source, he undertook a balloon flight on a day of total solar eclipse, and found no decrease in ionisation. He concluded that the air was ionised by something mysterious coming from outer space. The name 'cosmic rays' was suggested in 1925 by the American physicist Robert Millikan.

Cosmic rays are fast-moving elementary particles – mostly protons and atomic nuclei – that are produced in supernova explosions. They continually bombard Earth from all directions. We are well protected by the DNA-damaging effects of these rays by Earth's atmosphere and magnetic field.

1912
England

Our fake ancestor

Various British anthropologists

A forgery that fooled many of the greatest minds in science for four decades.

A skull – a blend of human and ape – was discovered in 1912 in a gravel pit in the Sussex village of Piltdown. It was described as a 500,000-year-old fossil and the proof of humans' ape-like ancestry – the 'missing link' between apes and humans that anthropologists have been searching for since Darwin postulated the existence of intermediate forms between ancestral apes and modern humans. Piltdown man was hailed by many British anthropologists as an ancestor of *Homo sapiens*. It was named *Eoanthropus dawsoni*, 'Dawson's dawn man', after Charles Dawson, a keen amateur archaeologist, who found the remains.

When fossils of *Australopithecus arfarensis*, a primitive hominid, were found in Africa in the 1930s, Piltdown man became an enigma. In 1953 chemical analysis and radiocarbon dating showed that the fossil was a fraud: the lower jaw was that of a female orang-utan deliberately coloured to look old; the skull was of human origin and was less than 1,000 years old.

Piltdown man is one of the greatest forgeries in the history of science. Thousands of textbooks had to be revised when this fake ancestor of humans was unmasked. The perpetrators of the fraud have never been identified. However, various people have come under suspicion, including Dawson, Sir Arthur Keith, an eminent anatomist who vigorously supported the idea that the fossil was indeed the 'missing link', and Sir Arthur Conan Doyle, the creator of Sherlock Holmes, who lived in Sussex and played golf at Piltdown.

See also THE FOSSIL CALLED LUCY, p. 173.

Watch your blood cholesterol level

1912
Russia

Nikolai Anichkov (1885–1964)

High blood cholesterol increases the risk of coronary heart disease, currently the world's most deadly disease.

'Watch your blood cholesterol level', is the mantra physicians preach to their older patients. Too much cholesterol in our bloodstream causes atherosclerosis, or the hardening of the arteries, which is responsible for a large proportion of heart attacks. There are two types of cholesterol: LDL (low-density lipoprotein), called 'bad' cholesterol because it's deposited on the artery walls and clogs them; HDL (high-density lipoprotein), called 'good' cholesterol because it unclogs the arteries. The higher your LDL level, the higher your risk of heart disease. But the higher your HDL level, the lower your risk.

Cholesterol, a molecule found in most animal tissues, is the most decorated molecule in history, having contributed to thirteen Nobel Prizes. But the work of the Russian scientist who first found the link between high levels of blood cholesterol and atherosclerosis wasn't even recognised by scientists outside Russia. Anichkov was a 27-year-old pathologist when he showed that rabbits fed on milk and egg yolks, a diet laden with cholesterol, developed atherosclerosis. In 1924 he refined his hypothesis: a high level of blood cholesterol, not cholesterol in food eaten, causes atherosclerosis.

The linking of cholesterol and atherosclerosis is now considered one of the greatest discoveries of Western medicine. Because Anichkov's research results were published only in Russian medical journals and because of the divide created by the Cold War, this great discovery didn't come to the attention of Western scientists for decades.

1913
Denmark

'It works even if you don't believe in it'

Niels Bohr (1885–1962)

The atom looks like a fuzzy cloud, not the familiar picture of electrons orbiting a tiny Sun-like nucleus.

Bohr, a major figure in 20th-century atomic physics, combined Rutherford's classical model of the atom (see p. 111) and Planck's quantum theory (see p. 96). He said that electrons can only be in fixed circular orbits. Each orbit has a specific amount of energy. The orbit closest to the nucleus is lowest in energy, with successively higher energies for more distant orbits. The energy of electrons is restricted to certain discrete values; that is, energy is quantised. This means only certain orbits are allowed. An electron can move from one orbit to another but can't occupy a position between orbits. Light is absorbed when an electron jumps to a higher orbit and emitted when an electron falls into a lower orbit.

Bohr's model is close to the modern quantum mechanics model, and the electrons aren't locked in precise orbits. Instead, the model gives the probability of finding them in different places near the nucleus. If the probability location of an electron is plotted in space, the plot looks like a fuzzy cloud extending over much of the atom.

According to I.B. Cohen, a well-known historian of physics, Bohr was fond of telling the story of a physicist who had a horse-shoe hanging on the door of his laboratory. When his colleagues asked whether he believed in such superstitions, the physicist replied: 'No, I don't believe in superstitions. But I have been told that it works even if you don't believe in it.'

ID for elements

Henry Moseley (1887–1915)

1913
England

The atomic number of an atom is the number of protons present in its nucleus.

The number of protons in the nucleus of every element is always the same. This means every element has a unique atomic number. As the atom is electrically neutral, the atomic number is also tells us the number of electrons in the atom. We usually write the atomic numbers as a subscript in front of the symbol of the atom. (The mass number of an atom – which is the sum of all protons and neutrons in its nucleus – is written as a superscript.)

We owe our knowledge of atomic numbers to Moseley, a brilliant chemist. After examining the spectra of 38 elements from aluminium to gold, he concluded that there was a 'fundamental quantity which increases by regular steps as we pass from one element to the next'. He identified this fundamental quantity as the charge on the proton. He'd discovered the Law of Atomic Numbers: the properties of elements are periodic functions of their atomic numbers. He prepared a new periodic table of elements based not on atomic weights – as done by Mendeleev (see p. 79) – but on atomic numbers. Although it didn't significantly change Mendeleev's table, it confirmed the positions of elements.

Moseley died at Gallipoli during the First World War at the age of 27. His life's work was done in less than four years. 'Before the world had heard of him, he was gone', notes Bernard Jaffe in his classic volume on the biographies of chemists, *Crucibles* (1957).

Setting the world on wheels

1913
USA

Henry Ford (1863–1947)

The idea of the moving assembly line wasn't Ford's, but he was the first to use it for the production of cars, so inventing mass production.

Ford, a car manufacturer who founded the Ford Motor Company in 1903, was determined to 'build a car for the great multitude ... so low in price that no man will be unable to own it'. He realised his dream in 1908 when he rolled out the Model T, or Tin Lizzie, as it was affectionately known. Before Model T, which was an instant hit, Ford built cars as every other manufacturer did – one at a time. Model T was cheap, but still not available to the 'great multitude'.

To produce cars more efficiently, he applied the four principles of mass production: division of labour, continuous flow, inter-changeable parts and reduction of wasted effort. The division of labour means dividing a complex job into several simple jobs. He broke down the complex process of assembling an engine into 84 separate operations. The job which had been done by one worker now required 84 workers, each doing one simple operation as a conveyor belt moved parts along the line of workers. The method increased the rate of production by four times. By 1913 all workers were trained to carry out various operations necessary to produce Model T in this new way, which reduced a car's assembly time from twelve hours to 93 minutes.

The last of more than 15 million Model Ts (which came out with Ford's famous promise: 'Any color – so long as it's black') was mass-produced in 1927.

Tossing the old views overboard

1915
Germany

Alfred Wegener (1880–1930)

Wegener was the first to suggest that the continents had once been joined together in a giant supercontinent.

Wegener, a meteorologist, called this supercontinent Pangaea (Greek for 'whole earth'). It began to break apart about 200 million years ago into the continents we know today, which slowly drifted into their current positions. The mountains were formed when the edges of two drifting continents were crumpled and folded; and the oceans when they moved away from each other.

Ever since Darwin proposed that species are related by descent, scientists believed that 'land bridges' once connected the continents. The bridges, which allowed the species to cross the oceans, sunk when the planet cooled and shrunk. The idea of a supercontinent started developing in Wegener's mind when he noticed the jigsaw-like fit between the coastlines of Africa and South America. He presented his theory in 1915 in his book, *The Origin of Oceans and Continents*. The book became the most controversial, derided and ridiculed book in the history of geology. Some prominent scientists labelled the book 'utter damned rot!', and questioned Wegener's 'scientific sanity'.

Part of the problem was that he never presented a convincing mechanism for his theory. Geologists discovered that mechanism in the 1960s and now Wegener's ideas are part of the theory of plate tectonics. The continents are still drifting apart, as suggested by Wegener, who believed: 'If it turns out that sense and meaning are now becoming evident … why should we hesitate to toss the old views overboard?'

Hooks and eyes of atoms

Gilbert Lewis (1875–1946)

A chemical bond is a strong force of attraction linking atoms in a molecule.

In his epic poem on the nature of the universe, the 1st-century-BC Roman poet Lucretius said that some atoms had hook-like projections and others eye-like ones, and that two atoms combine when the hook in one gets caught in the eye of the other. Gilbert, professor of chemistry at the University of California at Berkeley, made the first scientific effort to explain the union between two atoms.

The noble gases – helium neon, argon, krypton and xenon – all have a stable electronic configuration in their outermost or valence shells (eight electrons, except for helium which has two). The noble gases don't react with other elements; but other elements react because they have gaps in their valence shells. Lewis suggested that the complete transfer of valence shell electrons from one atom to another forms ionic bonds (for example, sodium gives an electron to chlorine to form sodium chloride). But when two atoms share electrons they form a covalent bond (for example, hydrogen and chlorine share a pair of electrons to form hydrogen chloride). In 1931 another American chemist, Linus Pauling, used quantum mechanics to explain Lewis's theory. He was awarded the 1954 Nobel Prize for Chemistry. Lewis is the only truly outstanding American scientist not to win a Nobel Prize. However, his chemical bonds are still taught in introductory chemistry courses.

Once during a lecture, Lewis was rudely interrupted by a question from a brilliant student. He reacted immediately: 'Young man, that was an impertinent question, but in the present connection it is entirely pertinent.'

A revolutionary moment in medicine

1921
Canada

Frederick Banting (1891–1941)

Insulin is the hormone responsible for the regulation of the sugar content of the blood; its deficiency results in the debilitating disease diabetes.

After returning from the First World War, Banting, an army surgeon, set up a practice and waited for patients. Only one patient visited in the first month. To make ends meet, he took up a teaching job. One night, while he was preparing for a lecture, he came across an article on the connection between the pancreas, the most important gland in digestion, and diabetes. Scientists knew that the removal of the pancreas in dogs produced diabetes, but weren't sure how it worked. Banting thought he could solve the problem. He jotted down notes for an experiment: 'Tie off pancreas ducts of dogs. Wait for six or eight weeks. Remove and extract.'

The next day he explained his ideas to J. J. R. McLeod, professor of physiology at the University of Toronto, and requested laboratory space, ten dogs and an assistant. As McLeod was in a hurry to go on holiday, he approved the plan. Banting and Charles Best, a graduate student, went to work on their dogs.

Within a few weeks, the duo achieved exciting results. But while the extract worked on dogs, would it work on humans? Banting and Best first injected the extract into each other to ensure it would cause no harm, and then into a fourteen-year-old boy dying of diabetes. The boy's blood sugar level returned to normal. Banting had successfully isolated insulin (a name suggested by McLeod) and, in doing so, he discovered a lifesaving treatment for people suffering from diabetes.

'Always a bridesmaid, but never a bride'

Gerard Lambert (1886–1967)

No, Lambert didn't discover halitosis, but his name is indelibly linked with it.

When an old employee of Lambert Pharmacal Company, makers of Listerine, saw a report on halitosis in the British medical journal *Lancet*, he mentioned it to Lambert, the son of the founder of the company. 'What's halitosis?' asked Lambert. 'Oh, that is the medical term for bad breath', replied the employee. Lambert seized upon the magic word as the basis for an advertising campaign for his company's mouthwash. The campaign played heavily on the effects of bad breath on people's lives (the pathetic case of 'Edna' who was 'always a bridesmaid, but never a bride' or the tragic case of the employee 'fired – and for a reason he never suspected') and sales skyrocketed.

Listerine was invented in 1879 by Lambert's father, a chemist, who managed to persuade Joseph Lister, the pioneer of antiseptic surgery (see p. 77), to grant him the right to christen his new product with the great man's name. Lambert, in his autobiography *All Out of Step* (1956), revealed: 'I have had the fear that my tombstone will bear the inscription, "Here lies the body of the Father of Halitosis".' There's no such inscription at his grave, but history does record him by this name.

Halitosis is not a modern condition. The affliction – and curing it with a mouthwash (originally of wine and herbs) – has been recorded as far back as 1550 BC. Oral bacteria, which produce foul-smelling gases such as hydrogen sulphide, cadaverine and putrescine, are the major cause of halitosis.

Little scientists discovering their own worlds

1923
Switzerland

Jean Piaget (1896–1980)

Piaget fundamentally changed the view of how children learn.

We show the child a tower of blocks on a table and ask him to build a second tower of the same height on another table (lower or higher than the first) with blocks of a different size. He begins to look around for a measuring standard, interestingly enough, the first measuring tool that comes to his mind is his own body. He puts one hand on top of his tower and the other at its base, and then, trying to keep his hands the same distance apart, he moves over to the other tower to compare it.

Piaget, the pioneering psychologist, who unravelled the mysteries of cognitive development to generations of teachers and parents, spent much of his professional life watching children learn (he wrote about the above experiment with a six-year-old boy in 1953). From such experiments, he divided cognitive development into four stages: (1) sensorimotor stage, 0–2 years; (2) preoperational stage, 2–6 years; (3) concrete operations, 6–11 years; and (4) formal operations, 11–adult.

He showed that, in the words of Seymour Papert, a prominent educator who worked with Piaget, 'children are not empty vessels to be filled with knowledge (as traditional pedagogical theory had it)'. Instead, they are 'active builders of knowledge – little scientists who are constantly creating and testing their own theories of the world'. Piaget published nearly 60 books; the first, *Moral Judgment of the Child*, in 1923. He was primarily interested in how knowledge developed in humans, what he called genetic epistemology.

A bizarre case

1925
USA

John Scopes (1900–70)

Scopes was charged with violating state law by teaching Darwin's theory of evolution.

Scopes, a 24-year-old high-school biology teacher, had assigned his pupils a simple task: reading five pages of a popular biology textbook dealing with evolution. He was charged with violating a State of Tennessee law that made it illegal to teach any theory that denies 'the Divine Creation of man as taught in Bible'.

The evolution–creationism trial turned the dusty little mining town of Dayton into a carnival. Banners decorated the street. Stalls sold 'Monkey Fizz' lemonade and 'Your Old Man's a Monkey' buttons. Chimpanzees were brought to town to 'testify' for the prosecution. About 1,000 people jammed the courthouse. After seven days of testimony and arguments between the prosecution ('If evolution wins, Christianity goes') and the defence ('Scopes isn't on trial; civilization is on trial') and eight minutes of deliberations by the judge, Scopes was found guilty and fined $100. A year later, the Tennessee Supreme Court overturned the verdict and dismissed the charges, concluding: 'Nothing is to be gained by prolonging the life of this bizarre case.'

After 80 years, evolution was again challenged in a US court. In 2004 the Dover Area School District in Pennsylvania directed teachers to preface the teaching of evolution with a disclaimer saying that evolution isn't a fact. After a 40-day evolution–Intelligent Design (ID) trial, the court ruled in 2005 that ID isn't a scientific theory but a repackaged creationism and banned the District 'from requiring teachers to denigrate or disparage the scientific theory of evolution'.

In the beginning

Georges Lemaître (1894–1966)

The universe began about 13.7 billion years ago in a hot, dense explosive state.

In the beginning was a black bomb
That blew apart. A blinding smoke
Kept growing, growing
To a tropical fog, intolerably bright.

That's how the British poet Edward Larrissy imagined the big bang in his 1994 poem. But scientists see it differently. In the beginning, the universe was infinitely dense and unimaginably hot. All matter, energy, time and space were formed at this instant. After 10^{-43} seconds the universe inflated from the size of an atom to that of a grapefruit. After 10^{-23} seconds the universe was a superhot soup (10^{27} °C) of electrons, quarks and other particles. The first atoms were formed after 380,000 years when the universe had cooled to 4,500°C, and the first stars and galaxies after 1 billion years when the temperature dropped to –200°C. The first stars have died now and the universe has cooled to –270°C (see p. 164).

Lemaître, a priest and an astronomer, was the first to propose that the universe was formed from a 'primeval atom'. When it exploded the fragments began to fly away from the explosion point, are still flying away now and will continue to do so indefinitely. In 1948 the American physicist George Gamow further elaborated Lemaître's theory.

What happened before the big bang? What caused the big bang? Scientists can't answer either of these questions because for them time only began with the big bang, and before that, there was nothing.

See also THE EXPANDING UNIVERSE, p. 130.

1927
Germany

For the love of locomotives

Werner Heisenberg (1901–76)

It's not possible to know simultaneously the exact position and momentum of a particle.

Nature has put a limit on the precision with which we can measure both the position and momentum (momentum is the mass times velocity) of a particle. The more precisely the position is determined, the less precisely the momentum is known, and vice versa. This is Heisenberg's famous uncertainty principle.

Heisenberg's formula for measuring uncertainty includes Planck's constant (see p. 96), an extremely small quantity. This means uncertainties play no part when we deal with matter on the macroscopic scale, such as the position and momentum of an automobile. But uncertainties become significant in the quantum world of atomic and subatomic particles where masses are extremely small. We can determine, for example, the exact location of an electron, but not its momentum (or energy) at the same time.

Once Heisenberg, who won the 1932 Nobel Prize for Physics, and one of his students were in deep scientific discussion while waiting for a train at a platform. When the train pulled up Heisenberg became intensely interested in its shiny new engine, but the student continued the discussion. 'Aren't you interested at all in this new type of locomotive?' Heisenberg asked the student. 'No, I'm only interested in theoretical physics', the student replied. 'Anyone who wishes to become a successful theoretical physicist must also become interested in locomotives', Heisenberg said curtly. The great physicist – who introduced uncertainty into our lives (for his principle has also changed the modern philosophical outlook) – was at least certain about something.

Driving Captain Kirk's Starship Enterprise

1928
England

Paul Dirac (1902–84)

All fundamental particles have a twin with the same mass but opposite charge.

In 1928 the electron and the proton were the only known fundamental particles. Physicists often wondered why electrons were always negatively charged and protons positively charged when the laws of physics were quite symmetrical in respect to charge. In his quantum theory of the electron, Dirac introduced a 'new kind of particle, unknown to experimental physics, having the same mass and opposite charge to an electron'. He called this particle antielectron (now known as the positron, short for positive electron). The symmetry between positive and negative charges in his theory also demanded an antiproton.

At first scientists were sceptical about the idea of positrons and antiprotons, but the discovery of positrons in cosmic rays in 1932 set the stage for the exotic world of antimatter. They now believe that all fundamental particles have an antimatter twin. When a particle collides with its antimatter twin they annihilate each other producing an awesome amount of energy. This energy drives *Star Trek*'s fictional Starship Enterprise.

Dirac – the 'purest soul in physics', as described by another gifted physicist Niels Bohr – was extremely reserved. A friend of Dirac once found him reading E. M. Forster's *A Passage to India* (1924). He knew the famous author and arranged a meeting between the two taciturn great minds. After introductions and tea there was a long silence and then Dirac asked: 'What happened in the cave?' Forster replied: 'I don't know.' Another long silence followed before they departed.

1928
England

The first wonder drug

Alexander Fleming (1881–1955)

Penicillin was the first antibiotic drug discovered.

Penicillin was discovered accidentally when Fleming, a Scottish bacteriologist, left a glass dish of *Staphylococcus* bacteria growing in a gelatine solution uncovered for several days. He found the dish contaminated with a bluish-green mould. He was about to discard the solution when he noticed that the bacteria were killed in areas surrounding the mould (moulds are very small plants and this brush-like mould was a rare species called *Penicillium notatum*, from the Latin *penicillius*, brush). After a few more experiments he confirmed that the mould was producing a substance that could kill bacteria but was harmless to other living things. He named the substance penicillin.

Fleming, however, was unsuccessful in isolating penicillin from the mould. In 1940 Australian pathologist Howard Florey and German–British biologist Ernst Chain produced the first pure penicillin at Oxford University in England. It was first tried on six patients in 1941. All responded well to treatment. Fleming, Florey and Chain were awarded the 1945 Nobel Prize for Physiology or Medicine.

During the Second World War penicillin was hailed as medicine's 'magic bullet' in the war against bacterial infections. Even now penicillin and other antibiotics (from Greek *anti*, 'against', and *bios*, 'life'; the term was first used in 1957) save millions of lives every year. Penicillin, one of the greatest medical breakthroughs in history, is still the most powerful antibiotic in existence. But antibiotics are now causing some concerns as their overuse might lead to the evolution of bacteria that are resistant to them.

Relax to generate alpha waves

1929
Germany

Hans Berger (1873–1941)

Berger was the first person to record electrical activity in the brain.

Berger was a psychiatrist at the University of Jena when he realised that the best way to study the human brain was neither by dissection nor psychoanalysis, the two methods known at that time, but by recording its electrical activity. Using a string galvanometer devised by Einthoven (see p. 101) he started experimenting on his patients. His early experiments were on patients who'd lost some of their skull bones in surgery. He made his first recordings in 1924 when he placed electrodes under the scalp of one of these patients. Later he succeeded in getting recordings from healthy people, including his teenage son.

A shy and aloof man, he worked in utmost secrecy for five years before he published his results. He reported that the brain generates rhythmic electrical impulses or 'brain waves'. He identified two types of waves: alpha waves (frequency 8 to 13 hertz or cycles per second) and beta waves (14 to 30 hertz). The waves change dramatically if the subject simply shifts from sitting quietly with eyes shut (alpha) to fully alert (beta). He called his recordings electro-encephalographs (Greek for 'the writing of the brain'). EEG is now the most widely used technique in neurology.

Initially, Berger's discovery was completely ignored in Germany. When he was introduced as the most distinguished of all the visitors at an international symposium in Paris, tears welled in his eyes as he said: 'In Germany I'm not so famous.' He died a lonely and dejected man.

1929
USA

Restoring the cosmic elegance

Edwin Hubble (1889–1953)

The universe isn't static; it's expanding – inflating like an unimaginably gigantic balloon.

Copernicus commanded Earth to move around the Sun, but his cosmos – and that of his followers Galileo, Newton and even Einstein – was static, and the Milky Way galaxy made up the entire cosmos. In the early 1920s Hubble, an astronomer at Mount Wilson Observatory in California, discovered other galaxies and proved that the universe extends beyond the edges of our galaxy.

Instead of resting on this Olympian laurel, Hubble ('an 'Olympian, tall, strong and beautiful with the shoulders of the Hermes of Praxiteles, and the benign serenity', in the words of his wife Grace, who idolised him) went on to show that these galaxies are moving away from us and each other at an ever-increasing rate. The more distant the galaxy, the faster it moves away from us. 'The discovery that the universe is expanding was one of the great intellectual revolutions of the twentieth century', remarked Stephen Hawking in *A Brief History of Time.*

The news of this revolution made Einstein ecstatic. Although his theory of general relativity didn't support the notion of a static universe, he accepted the idea. He fudged his equations by introducing a term he called the cosmological constant, a kind of 'anti-gravity' to balance gravity. In 1931 the humbled physicist visited the Mount Wilson Observatory and personally thanked Hubble, now a truly Olympian astronomer. A year later Einstein removed the cosmological constant – the biggest blunder of his career – from his general relativity equations and restored their cosmic elegance.

The little neutral ones

Wolfgang Pauli (1900–58)

1930
Austria

Neutrinos are elementary particles with no charge and are nearly massless.

Neutrinos travel at or near the speed of light. They are everywhere – trillions of them pass through our bodies each second – yet we can't see or feel them. They rarely interact with matter, and are the most elusive of all the elementary particles we know.

The idea of the neutrino was proposed by Pauli to explain the missing energy in the radioactive beta decay of an atomic nucleus in which a neutron turns into a proton and emits an electron. As the reaction seemed to violate the sacred law of the conservation of energy, Pauli suggested that a particle of zero charge and zero mass (it's now believed to have some mass) is released in such reactions. It takes the energy with it and disappears without trace. Pauli thought he'd made a terrible mistake, but in 1933 the Italian–American physicist Enrico Fermi proved his theory was correct (see p. 134). Fermi also christened the particle *il neutrino* ('the little neutral one'). Neutrinos were first detected in experiments in 1959.

The strange behaviour of neutrinos inspired the American novelist and poet John Updike to pen 'Cosmic Gall' (1959). An excerpt:

> *Neutrinos, they are very small.*
> *They have no charge and have no mass*
> *And do not interact at all.*
> *The earth is just a silly ball*
> *To them, through which they simply pass,*
> *Like dustmaids down a drafty hall*
> *Or photons through a sheet of glass.*

1931
Austria

Are there true things which can't be proved?

Kurt Gödel (1906–78)

All logical systems of any complexity are incomplete.

Every branch of mathematics has its own basic assumptions, known as axioms. Mathematicians like to derive everything from axioms. Gödel, an Austrian–American mathematician, suggested that in every logical system there would be some statements which were true but couldn't be proved according to its set of axioms. In other words, any such system would have more true statements than it can possibly prove.

One implication of Gödel's theorem is that a computer can never be as smart as the human brain. A computer can only operate by a given set of rules. It can never decide whether a statement is true if the statement can't be proved by its set of rules. The human brain, on the other hand, can recognise that the statement is true, even if it can't be proved logically.

Gödel was an eccentric and there are many anecdotes about him. Einstein and the economist Oskar Morgenstern, Gödel's closest friends in the US, accompanied him to the interview for his citizenship application. The officer was overwhelmed by this opportunity to talk to Einstein and discussed at length Nazi Germany. Eventually, he turned to Gödel and said: 'But of course from your reading of the Constitution you know that nothing like that could happen here.' Gödel, the brilliant abstract logician who could find logical flaws in any document, replied: 'As a matter of fact …' Morgenstern kicked him under the table to stop him babbling about the Constitution. Gödel got his citizenship.

Turning coffee into theorems

1933
Hungary

Paul Erdös (1913–96)

Chebyshev's theorem states that for every number greater than 1, there's always a prime number (a number divisible by itself or by 1) between it and its double.

The Russian mathematician Pafnuty Chebyshev proved in 1850 the theorem that now bears his name. Erdös, when he was only twenty, provided a far more elegant proof for the famous result. This achievement marked the beginning of an extraordinary career in mathematics. Erdös is believed to be the most prolific mathematician in history. He published more than 1,500 papers (a really great mathematician may publish 50 papers in a lifetime) and collaborated with about 460 mathematicians, who all have what mathematicians affectionately call Erdös number 1. A mathematician earned this moniker when he or she published a paper with him. Some 4,500 mathematicians have Erdös number 2: they have published with someone who published with Erdös, and so on.

Erdös was a true eccentric, and mathematics was his life. He never owned anything ('property is nuisance', he used to say) except for two suitcases, each half-full. For 50 years he wandered the globe staying with mathematicians. In return for their hospitality, he showered them with problems and rare mathematical insights. He won many awards, but gave away the prize money as rewards for solving problems.

To him, a mathematician was a machine for turning coffee into theorems. And there were three steps in the mental degradation of a mathematician. First you forget your theorems. Next you forget to zip up. Last you forget to zip down.

'And this is Fermi's theory of beta decay'

Enrico Fermi (1901–54)

Beta decay is a nuclear reaction in which a neutron is converted into a proton, an electron and a neutrino.

Beta decay is a very common form of the disintegration of radioactive nuclei. The net effect of beta decay is that the number of neutrons decreases by one and the number of protons increases by one. For example, unstable radioactive carbon-14 (eight neutrons, six protons) decays into stable nitrogen-14 (seven neutrons, seven protons). This process is known as transmutation of elements. The fast-moving electrons emitted in beta decay are called beta particles, which can be harmful to humans, especially if ingested or inhaled.

When Fermi submitted his paper on beta decay to the prestigious journal *Nature*, the editor rejected it because it 'contained speculations which were too remote from reality'. Fermi, a genius ahead of his time, was forced to flee Mussolini's Italy (his wife Laura was Jewish) soon after receiving the 1938 Nobel Prize for Physics. In 1942 he produced the first man-made nuclear chain reaction at the University of Chicago.

Emilio Segrè, who shared the 1959 Nobel Prize for Physics, recalled in his book, *Enrico Fermi, Physicist* (1970):

> After attending a seminar given by one of Oppenheimer's pupils on Fermi's beta-ray theory, Fermi met me and said: 'Emilio, I am getting rusty and old, I cannot follow the highbrow theory developed by Oppenheimer's pupils anymore. I went to their seminar and was depressed by my inability to understand them. Only the last sentence cheered me up; it was: "And this is Fermi's theory of beta decay."'

See also FERMI'S PARADOX, p. 150.

Whispers from space

Karl Jansky (1905–50)

1933
USA

Radio astronomy is the study of radio waves that reach Earth from outer space.

When 23-year-old Jansky joined the Bell Labs in 1928 as a radio engineer, the recently opened New York-to-London radio telephone service was plagued with the intermittent noisy crackling of static interference. Bell Labs engineers were interested in reducing noise levels in telephone conversations. Jansky's job was to record the intensity of this interference with a radio receiver connected to an antenna – a long array of metal pipes – mounted on four Ford Model T wheels. An electric motor moved the wheels on a large sprocket to point the antenna to any part of the sky. During one of his experiments Jansky heard a steady hissing sound, which was very different from the intermittent crackling of the static. He had the insight to realise that the sound wasn't of terrestrial origin. He soon discovered that the signals were indeed coming from the centre of the Milky Way.

The young engineer had accidentally opened a new way of looking at the universe; but scientists, including Jansky, failed to appreciate the significance of this discovery.

There was one man, however, who understood the possibilities of radio astronomy. This was a 22-year-old engineering student named Grote Reber. Inspired by Jansky's discovery, he immediately decided to build a visionary bowl-shaped antenna, nine metres in diameter, in his backyard. Using this first true radio telescope, for nearly a decade he conducted an extensive survey of the sky and produced the first maps of radio sources in the galaxy.

See also PULSARS, p. 166.

Changing behaviour under pressure

Eugene Wigner (1902–95) and Hillard Huntington (d. 1992)

Hydrogen is the simplest and most abundant of all elements.

Hydrogen has no obvious position in the periodic table of elements. There are good chemical reasons for placing it with alkali metals such as lithium and sodium. Like them, it has only one electron in the outer shell and loses this electron when it enters into chemical combination with other elements. But hydrogen is a gas and not a metal. On the other hand, many of its properties resemble those of halogens such as fluorine and chlorine. Like them, it can also gain an electron when forming compounds.

Why is hydrogen's behaviour so eccentric? The chemical properties of an element are shown when it combines with other elements. The element then loses or gains electrons. When hydrogen loses its lone electron, all that remains is a proton – the hydrogen nucleus has no neutron. In the case of other elements the atom still has some electrons surrounding the nucleus. Hence the chemistry of hydrogen is the only chemistry of its kind.

In 1935 Wigner and Huntington, Princeton University physicists, enhanced understanding of hydrogen when they proposed that under enormous pressure hydrogen molecules, which contain two atoms each, would break up and recombine as a lattice of single atoms that could conduct electricity. Scientists have succeeded in producing metallic hydrogen in the laboratory, but only for a few microseconds. The potential uses of metallic hydrogen are fascinating to contemplate, but they are far down the road. It's also been suggested that metallic hydrogen may be a superconductor at room temperature.

Cosmic mirage

Fritz Zwicky (1898–1974)

1937
USA

An effect caused by the gravity of a massive galaxy or a cluster of galaxies focusing light that passes it.

Einstein's theory of general relativity says that gravity can bend light. For example, when a star's light passes the Sun, it's bent towards Earth by the Sun's gravity. This phenomenon was confirmed when scientists viewed light from stars located behind the Sun during the total solar eclipse of 1919.

In 1937 Zwicky, a gifted observational astronomer at the California Institute of Technology, suggested the gravitational-lens effects of galaxies: that the light coming from a faraway galaxy may be deflected by galaxies in front of it. However, Einstein concluded that 'there is no great chance of observing this phenomenon'. This comment from the great man killed the idea of gravitational lenses. The idea was revived in 1979 when astronomers discovered a double quasar (quasars are the very bright centres of some distant galaxies). The two quasars were so close that astronomers suspected that a gravitational lens might be producing twin images of a single quasar. Later observations showed a cluster of galaxies was blocking the direct view of the quasar.

Zwicky was a colourful character and there are many stories about him, mostly embellished. His pet insult was 'spherical bastards' (bastards any way you look at them). He was once discussing the beginning of the universe with a priest. When the priest said that the universe began when God said 'Let there be light', Zwicky replied that he would accept the statement if it could be changed to: 'Let there be electromagnetism.'

The cause of mosquitoes' sorrow

1939
Switzerland

Paul Hermann Müller (1899–1965)

DDT is effective in controlling insect pests that cause diseases such as typhus and malaria and destroy vegetation.

Arsenic-based pesticides were widely used in the early 20th century, but they were highly toxic to humans and other mammals. Müller, a chemist, was working on developing an alternative to these pesticides when he discovered that DDT – the short name of an organic compound synthesised in 1874 by a German chemist, Othmar Ziedler – was a highly effective pesticide.

In the early 1940s the United States government conducted studies to determine the effects of DDT on human health and concluded that it was relatively harmless. Soon DDT became the most popular pesticide throughout the world, and Müller was awarded the 1948 Nobel Prize for Physiology or Medicine.

The popularity of DDT led an unknown wit to write the following limerick:

> *A mosquito was heard to complain*
> *A chemist has poisoned my brain.*
> *The cause of his sorrow*
> *was paradichloro-*
> *diphenyl-trichloroethane.*

However, the overuse of DDT for commercial and agricultural purposes soon resulted in the contamination of soil and water. In turn, DDT started passing through the food chain and toxic levels of DDT were detected in humans and animals. The US government banned its use in the late 1960s. The moral of the story: too much of a good thing can become the cause of our own sorrow.

See also SILENT SPRING, p. 161.

How the Sun shines

Hans Bethe (1906–2005)

1939
USA

Nuclear fusion in the Sun is the source of its energy and ours.

Stars like the Sun are simply balls of burning gases. The Sun is composed of 70 per cent hydrogen, 28 per cent helium and a sprinkling of other elements. Its surface temperature is 6,000°C, but its interior burns at 15 million °C. At this temperature, atomic nuclei are stripped of their electrons, moving freely among the electrons themselves. Occasionally two hydrogen nuclei (two protons) combine to form a deuterium nucleus (one proton, one neutron), producing energy in the process. When another proton collides with a deuterium nucleus, they combine to form helium-3 (two protons, one neutron). Finally, two helium-3 nuclei combine to form stable helium-4 (two protons, two neutrons).

These types of reactions in which lighter nuclei combine to form a heavier nucleus are called nuclear fusions (a nuclear fission, on the other hand, is the breaking up of a heavy nucleus into two or more lighter nuclei). In his classic paper, 'Energy Production in Stars', Bethe explained how the stars get their energy. He was awarded the 1967 Nobel Prize for Physics for his work

Bethe joined Cornell University in 1935 after fleeing Nazi Germany. He lived and taught at Cornell for almost 70 years. He came every day to eat lunch at the student cafeteria, recalls Freeman Dyson, who was a student of Bethe. 'Everyone called him Hans. He told us that one of the best things about moving from Germany to America was that nobody in America called him "Herr Professor".'

Element 118 and counting

1940
USA

Edwin McMillan (1907–91)
and Philip Abelson (1913–2004)

Elements heavier than uranium are called transuranium elements.

Uranium (element 92; it has 92 protons), is the heaviest element known to exist naturally in detectable amounts on earth. Elements beyond uranium in the periodic table of elements are all artificially produced, short-lived and radioactive.

The first artificial element was created by McMillan and Abelson at the Lawrence Berkeley Laboratory in California. They bombarded uranium with extremely fast-moving neutrons, the uranium nuclei absorbed the neutrons and turned into neptunium (element 93), a short-lived and radioactive element. Scientists have so far created most of the other elements between neptunium and element 118.

Four laboratories are at the forefront of creating elements: Lawrence Berkeley, the Lawrence Livermore National Laboratory in California, GSI at Darmstadt in Germany, and the Joint Institute of Nuclear Research at Dubna, near Moscow. They all use expensive cyclotron or synchrotron, particle accelerators that allow particles to be accelerated to speeds close to the speed of light. During the Cold War a group of United States legislators visited the Dubna laboratory. A Soviet physicist asked one of the visitors how they got their money to build their accelerators. The visitor explained the long legislative process of getting money. 'That is not the way I understand', the physicist said. 'I understand you get it by saying the Russians have a 10-billion electron volt synchrotron and we need a 20-billion electron volt synchrotron and that is how you get your money.' The US legislator asked: 'How do you get your money?' He replied: 'The same way.'

The forgotten woman of physics

Lise Meitner (1878–1968)

Meitner was the co-discoverer of nuclear fission, but was denied a share in the 1944 Nobel Prize.

In 1938 the German chemist Otto Hahn made a startling discovery: uranium nuclei bombarded with slow-moving neutrons gave barium. He wrote to Meitner – a long-time associate who had fled Nazi Germany to escape the persecution of Jews and was living in exile in Sweden – to help him find an explanation for his discovery. Within a few weeks, she worked out the theoretical interpretation of the effect we now know as nuclear fission. Hahn published the chemical evidence for nuclear fission without listing Meitner as a co-author. In 1944 he was awarded the Nobel Prize for Chemistry for his work.

Meitner didn't get a share in the Nobel Prize. She was used to such disappointments. She was an Austrian Jew in Hitler's Germany, a female in the male world of physics, unmarried when society frowned upon career women. In her day, Meitner was Germany's best experimental physicist. Einstein, who very briefly worked with Meitner, fondly referred to her as 'our Marie Curie'.

Hahn had always maintained that discovery of nuclear fission was solely the result of chemical experiments done by him and his assistant Fritz Strassmann after Meitner had left Germany. But new evidence shows the details of his correspondence with Meitner and the importance of Meitner's intellectual leadership in the discovery of nuclear fission. Though she was denied a share in the Nobel Prize, Meitner has now been rewarded with a far more durable fame: the element 109, meitnerium (Mt), honours her name.

1944
Ireland

The book that helped unlock the secret of life

Erwin Schrödinger (1887–1961)

What Is Life? **is considered one of the most influential books of the 20th century.**

In 1944 Schrödinger, the celebrated Austrian physicist famous for his thought experiment, known as Schrödinger's cat, published a book, *What Is Life?* In this 'little book' (as he self-deprecatingly called it), he speculated that life's genetic information had to be compact enough to be stored in molecules in 'some kind of code-script'. These molecules, passed from parent to child, are 'the material carrier of life'.

He said that unlike a crystal, the hereditary substance doesn't repeat itself. He called this an aperiodic crystal. 'We believe a gene – or perhaps the whole chromosome fibre – to be an aperiodic solid', he said. 'Aperiodic crystal, in my opinion, is the material carrier of life.' The aperiodic nature of the hereditary molecule would allow it to encode a large amount of genetic information with a small number of atoms, he suggested. Schrödinger, who was awarded the 1933 Nobel Prize for Physics, wrote *What Is Life?* during his sixteen years at the Institute of Advanced Studies in Dublin, Ireland.

Schrödinger's book – which is now copyright-free and available on the internet – inspired many young scientists to study molecular biology. Francis Crick and James Watson have both acknowledged how the book inspired them. 'This book very elegantly propounded the belief that genes were the key components of living cells and that, to understand what life is, we must know how genes act', Watson wrote in his memoir *The Double Helix* (1968).

Processing instructions one after another

1945
USA

John von Neumann (1903–57)

**All stored-program computers have a memory (hard disk)
to store programs and data and a calculating and control unit
(central processor) for executing instructions.**

Like all early computers, the world's first digital computer, ENIAC,
was capable of doing only one task at a time (legend has it that
ENIAC's 18,000 vacuum tubes consumed so much electricity that
whenever it was turned on, it dimmed the lights of Philadelphia).
For a different task, it had to be reprogrammed manually by resetting
switches and rewiring. The Hungarian-born von Neumann, a brilliant mathematician, was a consultant to both ENIAC (completed
in 1946) and its successor EDVAC (completed in 1952). In 1945 he
published a report on EDVAC in which he outlined a new concept
for the computer which would allow it to perform different tasks
without any changes to hardware. The concept came to be known
as stored-program computing or von Neumann architecture.

Von Neumann was a legend in his own time. He was famous
for his extraordinary photographic memory. He once said that he
knew all the numbers in the Manhattan telephone directory – the
only thing he needed, to be able to dispense with the book alto-
gether, was to know the names that the numbers belonged to. He
explained a car accident in this way: 'I was proceeding down the
road. The trees on the right were passing me in orderly fashion at
60 miles per hour. Suddenly one of them stopped in my path.
Boom!'

Most computers today use von Neumann architecture, which
let instructions pass in an orderly fashion without stopping.

1946
USA

The radiocarbon revolution

Willard Libby (1908–80)

Radiocarbon dating is a technique to measure the age of organic materials.

Atmospheric carbon dioxide contains three types of carbon: about 99 per cent ordinary carbon-12, about 1 per cent carbon-13, and about one atom in a trillion of radioactive carbon-14. All animals and plants absorb carbon dioxide and, therefore, contain a fixed amount of carbon-14 relative to carbon-12. But when they die, this ratio starts changing as carbon-14 in the tissue decays into carbon-12. The rate of decay is constant, and by finding the proportion of carbon-14 in organic remains, it can be determined how long ago they died.

Willard Libby, a chemist at the University of Chicago, discovered the technique to measure carbon-14 in organic materials, for which he won the 1960 Nobel Prize for Chemistry. Radiocarbon dating 'may indeed help roll back the pages of history and reveal to mankind something more about his ancestors, and in this way perhaps about his future', he noted in his Nobel lecture.

Radiocarbon dating has revolutionised archaeology. For example, in 1947 a young Bedouin shepherd searching for a stray goat entered a long-untouched cave and found jars filled with thousands of ancient scrolls. Historical evidence suggested that the manuscripts, now known as Dead Sea Scrolls, were written during biblical and early Jewish times. But many scholars questioned whether they were genuine. Radiocarbon dating of a small sample from one of the scrolls gave it a date of 100 BC, proving that they were indeed ancient.

See also THE SHROUD OF TURIN, p. 184.

The whole picture

Dennis Gabor (1900–79)

1947
UK

Holography is a method of recording the image of an object on a photographic film by a laser beam. The image – known as a hologram – looks three-dimensional to the naked eye.

A photographic film, like our eyes, records only the intensity of a light wave. It doesn't record different phases of the wave as it oscillates through a 360-degree cycle from crest to trough. A hologram is made by two light beams. One beam goes straight from the source to the film; the other beam first hits the object, which scatters the light changing its phase. Both beams leave an image on the film simultaneously. Because these light beams carry phase information, the combined image has the whole information about the object.

Hungarian-born Gabor said the idea for holography 'came out of my unconsciousness' as he waited for his turn for a tennis court. He coined the term 'holograph' from the Greek *holographos* (*holos*, 'whole' and *graphos*, 'writing'), because holography records the whole message of a light wave. Gabor's holograms were made by using two mercury vapour lamps as the light source. As light from these lamps was not coherent (of single colour or wavelength), his holograms contained distortions. The invention of the laser in 1960 revived holography.

Gabor, who won the 1971 Nobel Prize for Physics, once remarked: 'You can't predict the future but you can invent it.' Holography has helped invent the future in many ways; for example, X-ray holography is now used to record three-dimensional images of internal parts of the body.

They came out in the wash

Barbara McClintock (1902–92)

Jumping genes are strands of DNA that are capable of moving between chromosomes.

There was no morning call from Stockholm; Barbara McClintock does not have a phone. Instead, the 81-year-old geneticist learned the news by radio. 'Oh, dear,' she is said to have murmured. And having pronounced that judgment, the diminutive scientist donned her usual attire – baggy dungarees, a man-tailored shirt and sturdy oxfords – and stepped out for her usual morning walk through the woods …

With these words *Time* magazine (24 October 1983) recorded the gentle geneticist's reaction to receiving the 1983 Nobel Prize for physiology or medicine, and thus becoming the first woman to receive the first unshared medicine Nobel.

After spending years carefully breeding and crossbreeding corn, McClintock noticed that colour changes in the successive generations of corn didn't follow predictable hereditary patterns. She soon discovered that these changes were due to strings of DNA which had the ability to cut and paste themselves into different chromosomes. Geneticists ignored the discovery for more than two decades, as they then knew very little about the DNA. 'They thought I was crazy, absolutely mad', she recalled later. But it didn't worry her: 'When you know you're right, you don't care what others think. You know sooner or later it will come out in the wash.'

At last, the significance of jumping genes (formally called transposons) in genetics research has done exactly that. Researchers, among other things, are using jumping genes to create transgenic insects, which may help stop some infectious diseases and benefit agriculture.

When the stomach's feedback failed

Norbert Wiener (1894–1964)

Cybernetics is the science of control and communication in both machines and living things.

'Once in a great while a scientific book is published that sets bells jangling wildly in a dozen different sciences', a reviewer noted on the publication of Wiener's seminal book, *Cybernetics* (1948). The book introduced what was both a new word (from the Greek *kubernētēs*, meaning 'steersman'), and an entirely new field of science. Wiener wanted to find 'the common elements in the functioning of automatic machines and the human nervous system', to prepare us for the new 'automated age' ('to live effectively is to live with adequate information').

Wiener's book also introduced the terms 'input', 'output' and 'feedback' which are now part of our everyday vocabulary. Feedback – controlling the performance of a system by using output to modify its input – is a fundamental concept in cybernetics. The familiar thermostat works on this principle. Wiener said that by copying the control mechanism of the human brain, we can build better machines. His book led to the beginning of artificial intelligence research in the 1950s.

Wiener – described as a baroque figure, short, rotund, myopic, bearded and kindly – spent most of his professional life at the Massachusetts Institute of Technology. One day he was walking across the campus when a student stopped him with a question. After Wiener had explained the answer, the student thanked him and started walking away. 'Just one moment', said Wiener. 'Which way was I walking when we met?' The student pointed the direction that Wiener had been headed. 'Good', said Wiener. 'Then I have had my lunch.'

1949
UK

The importance of professors

Alexander Todd (1907–97)

Nucleotides are the basic building blocks of DNA and RNA.

Nucleotides are made up of a five-carbon atom sugar in ring form (ribose or deoxyribose), phosphoric acid and a nitrogen-containing base: adenine (A), cytosine (C), guanine (G), thymine (T) or uracil (U). Four types of nucleotides are found in DNA and RNA, differing only in the nitrogen-containing base: A, C, G and T in DNA; A, C, G and U in RNA.

Todd, who was awarded the 1957 Nobel Prize for Chemistry for this work, was a heavy smoker. In his memoirs, *A Time to Remember: The Autobiography of a Chemist* (1983), he recounts an occasion, going back to wartime years of shortages, when he found himself without any cigarettes while he was at a defence chemical works. He hastened to the officers' bar and asked the barman rather timidly:

'Can I have some cigarettes?'

'What's your rank?' was the slightly unexpected reply.

'I'm afraid I haven't got one,' I answered.

'Nonsense – everyone who comes here has a rank.'

'I'm sorry but I just don't have one.'

'Now that puts me in a spot,' said the barman, 'for orders about cigarettes in this camp are clear – twenty for officers and ten for other ranks. Tell me what exactly are you?'

Now I really wanted those cigarettes so I drew myself up and said 'I am the Professor of Chemistry at Manchester University.' The barman contemplated me for about thirty seconds and then said 'I'll give you five.'

Since that day I have had few illusions about the importance of professors!

Should I take the umbrella, dear?

1949
USA

Edward A. Murphy Jr (1918–90)

Murphy's law has many variations, but the standard statement is: 'If anything can go wrong, it will.'

Life's little annoyances – such as being unable to find a matching pair of socks, or taking along an umbrella that turned out to be unneeded or not taking one when it was needed – caused James Payne, a Victorian satirist, to lament in 1884:

> *I never had a piece of toast*
> *Particularly long and wide*
> *But fell upon the sanded floor*
> *And always on the buttered side.*

These little annoyances acquired a 'scientific' name, Murphy's law, when Captain Murphy of the United States Air Force came across a gauge that had been wired wrongly. He cursed the technician responsible and muttered something like: 'If anything can go wrong, it will.'

Murphy's law occurs too frequently to be pure chance. Haven't you noticed that whenever you are trying to park your car along a busy road, all the empty spaces are on the other side; or that the supermarket checkout queue you joined moves slower than the one next to you? Robert A. J. Matthews, a British physicist, believes that Murphy's law isn't just nonsense. It can be explained by scientific principles. In 1995 he showed, in five pages of mathematical equations, why toast usually lands with the buttered side down. And after years of research he's still complaining that today's highly accurate weather forecasts are still not good enough to prove Murphy's law of umbrellas ('Carrying an umbrella when rain is forecast makes rain less likely to fall') wrong.

Where is everybody?

Enrico Fermi (1901–54)

1950
USA

If there's intelligent extraterrestrial life, why aren't they here?

At a lunch in the summer of 1950 at Los Alamos Laboratory, Fermi (see p. 134) and fellow nuclear physicists Konopinski, Edward Teller and Herbert York were talking about space travel. The discussion was probably prompted by a recent cartoon in the *New Yorker* magazine explaining why rubbish bins were disappearing from the streets of the city. The cartoon showed 'little green men' with antennae carrying rubbish bins towards a flying saucer. The discussion veered towards the possibility of many civilisations beyond Earth. Fermi surprised everyone by asking the provocative question: If they are there, why aren't they here? This is Fermi's paradox.

There are many explanations: *serious* (evolutionary biologist Ernst Mayr: the evolution path that leads to intelligent life is far more complex than we suppose – we're, if not the first, then among the first intelligent life forms to evolve in the galaxy; astronomer Carl Sagan: daunting distances of interstellar space make space travel impossible … if we are alone in the universe, it sure seems like an awful waste of space); *bizarre* (astronomer John A. Ball's zoo hypothesis which portrays Earth as a zoo of an intelligent life in the galaxy – they're watching us from a distance); *humorous* (science writer Arthur C. Clarke: 'I'm sure the universe is full of intelligent life – it's just been too intelligent to come here'); and *optimistic* (astronomer Frank Drake: 'They could show up here tomorrow').*

For various explanations and implications of Fermi's paradox, see the author's Why Aren't They Here?: The Question of Life on Other Worlds *(Icon Books, 2007).*

The absorbing atoms

Alan Walsh (1916–98)

The atomic absorption spectrophotometer uses the light absorbed by atoms to measure trace elements in a sample.

On a sunny Sunday morning Walsh was working in his vegetable garden when he suddenly had a revealing thought. Ecstatic with joy he hurried inside and phoned his colleague, John Shelton. 'Look John!' he exulted. 'We've been measuring the wrong bloody thing! We should be measuring absorption, not emission!'

For years Walsh, a physicist, had been searching for an answer to a problem that had eluded scientists for nearly a century: how trace elements (small concentrations of elements present in a sample) could be measured by spectroscopy. In spectroscopy a minute quantity of the liquid sample solution is sprayed into a flame that vaporises the solution releasing metal elements from their compounds. A beam of light passes through the flame and a device on the other side measures the spectrum. So far he'd been measuring light emitted by the atoms. That Sunday morning flash of inspiration told him that he should be measuring light that had been absorbed by the atoms. Early the next morning Walsh set up a simple experiment using the element sodium. Within hours he had a successful result. This experiment transformed the humble spectroscope into an extraordinarily sensitive device which, of course, deserved a grand name.

Atomic absorption spectrophotometers are now standard equipment in factories, laboratories and hospitals, where they are used to measure concentrations of about 70 different metallic elements present as traces in substances as diverse as soil, blood, urine, wine, petroleum and minerals.

1952
USA

How not to become a pseudoscientist

Martin Gardner (b. 1914)

Pseudoscience is ideas and beliefs, such as astrology and phrenology, which masquerade as science, but have no or little relationship to scientific method. Theories of real science are continually being added to and updated, but the ideologies of pseudoscience are fixed.

Gardner is a well-known author of numerous books and a relentless fighter against pseudoscience. His 1952 book, *In the Name of Science* (which was republished in 1957 as *Fads and Fallacies in the Name of Science*), launched the modern sceptical movement. In this book he lists five characteristics of pseudoscientists.

- They consider themselves geniuses.
- They regard other scientists as ignorant blockheads.
- They believe themselves unjustly persecuted and discriminated against because recognised scientific societies refuse to let them lecture and peer-reviewed journals ignore their research papers or assign them to 'enemies' to review them.
- Instead of sidestepping the mainstream science, they have strong compulsions to focus on the greatest scientists and best-established theories. For example, according to the laws of science a perpetual motion machine cannot be built. A pseudoscientist builds one.
- They often write in complex jargon, in many cases using terms and phrases they themselves have coined. Even on the subject of the shape of Earth, you may find it difficult to win a debate with a pseudoscientist who argues that Earth is flat.

Simply put, a pseudoscientist believes that their hypothesis can never be wrong, but a real scientist always welcomes new ideas as these ideas give them the opportunity to test their hypothesis in new situations.

'We have found the secret of life'

1953
UK

Francis Crick (USA, 1916–2004) and James Watson (UK, b. 1928)

DNA consists of a double helix of two strands coiled around each other.

Crick and Watson were two young and unknown scientists when they solved the puzzle of the structure of DNA at the Cavendish Laboratory in Cambridge. One afternoon Crick walked into the Eagle pub in Cambridge and announced: 'We have found the secret of life.' That morning they'd discovered the last piece of the puzzle that revealed the double helix structure of DNA. In short, when the two strands of the double helix are uncoiled, they can produce two copies of the original. This unique structure explains how DNA stores genetic information and how it passes this on to the next generation by making an identical copy of itself.

A DNA (deoxyribonucleic acid) molecule is like a twisted ladder. Each 'side of the ladder' is made up of chains of alternating sugar and phosphate units. 'Rungs' are made from pairs of four chemical compounds called bases: adenine (A), thymine (T), cytosine (C) and guanine (G). The bases always pair in a specific manner: A pairs with T, and C pairs with G. Thus there are only four combinations possible: A–T, C–G, T–A and G–C. The genetic code is the sequence of bases along the length of DNA.

DNA's twisted ladder is an icon of our times. Many of today's science breakthroughs heralded in media headlines, from cloning to gene therapy, have their origins in Crick and Watson's discovery, which won them the 1962 Nobel Prize for Physiology or Medicine.

See also GENETIC (OR DNA) FINGERPRINTING, p. 181.

1953
USA

A bolt of lightning,
and there was life

Stanley Miller (b. 1930)

The experiment to create biomolecules by physical processes aimed to prove the idea that the emergence of life on Earth wasn't an accident; it was inevitable.

According to the current textbook picture, life originated in a primitive ocean 3.8 billion years ago. This primordial soup contained all the ingredients necessary to form information-carrying molecules able to self-replicate, mutate and evolve. Darwin suggested in 1871 that life arose in a 'warm little pond' where a prebiotic broth of organic chemicals, over millions of years, might have given rise to the first organisms. In the 1930s the Russian scientist A. I. Oparin and the British scientist J. B. S. Haldane refined this idea independently.

In 1953 Stanley Miller, a young graduate student working in the laboratory of the Nobel Prize-winning chemist Harold Urey at the University of Chicago provided the first experimental support to the primordial soup theory. He subjected a mixture of methane, ammonia, water vapour and hydrogen to a series of electrical charges. He imagined this to be a rough duplication of conditions on the primitive Earth when the primordial soup was subjected to bolts of lightning. After a week, the inorganic molecules had joined to form several amino acids, the building blocks of proteins.

In 2006 Xiang Zhang and Scot Martin of Harvard University conducted an experiment in which they successfully ran parts of the Krebs cycle – a complex cycle of key metabolic reactions – in reverse. Their experiment brings scientists a step closer to creating life in a test tube.

The clock's still ticking

Clair Patterson (1922–95)

1955

USA

Patterson provided the first reliable age of Earth: about 4.55 billion years.

In 1650 James Ussher, Archbishop of Armagh in Ireland, calculated that, according to biblical accounts, Earth was created on Sunday, 23 October 4004 BC. In 1897 the English physicist Lord Kelvin made the first scientific estimate for the age of Earth by assuming that it originally was a hot solid sphere. By calculating the rate of cooling, he arrived at an age of 100 million years. Geologists, however, thought that Earth was considerably older. When Patterson, a geochemist at the California Institute of Technology, started his measurements in the 1950s, geologists believed that Earth was a few billion years old.

Geologists find out the age of rocks by reading the radioactive clock that ticks away in every rock as traces of radioactive atoms decay into non-radioactive stable atoms. The ratio of radioactive and stable atoms tells how fast the clock was ticking. The actual amount of the radioactive atoms tells how long that clock had been running. Stony meteorites contain traces of radioactive lead, which must have been present in the meteorite when it was formed from the primordial cloud of gas that became our solar system. Patterson studied the rate of decay of radioactive lead in these meteorites to work out the age of Earth.

Patterson subsequently turned his attention from lead in meteorites to lead in the atmosphere. His crusade against lead pollution from automobiles made him the model for Sam Beech in Saul Bellow's novel *The Dean's December* (1982).

Chicken Little's warning

Eugene Shoemaker (1928–97)

Shoemaker was the first to alert the world to the dangers of meteorite impacts.

The world's first authenticated and best-preserved impact crater is in Arizona. Known simply as the Meteor Crater, its rim-to-rim diameter is 1.2 kilometres and its depth below the surrounding plain is about 175 metres. Today we know that it was gouged out about 50,000 years ago by a meteorite with a diameter roughly the width of a football field – but in the early 1950s most geologists believed that it was formed by a volcano.

Shoemaker, a geologist, was probing the crater when he found a type of silica that's formed only by tremendous impact. The impact shatters rocks throwing tiny grains of quartz into the air. The shattering is so violent that it leaves patterns on these grains, known as shocked quartz. He subsequently found the same telltale quartz in other craters. He began to form the theory that both the Meteor Crater and the craters on the Moon were due to the impacts of meteorites. In 1960 he received his doctorate from Princeton University for his seminal research on the mechanics of meteorite impacts.

He warned that it was only a matter of time before Earth would be struck again. When his warning was ignored he remarked in 1994: 'Nobody believed Chicken Little when he said that the sky was falling. But occasionally the sky does fall, and with horrendous effects.' Three years later he was killed in a car accident while hunting for impact craters in Australia's outback.

Through the looking glass

Chen Ning Yang (b. 1922) and Tsung-Dao Lee (b. 1926)

Mirror matter is no longer the stuff of science fiction.

The idea of antiparticles (see p. 127) leads to the idea of symmetry, but in 1956 Chinese–American physicists Yang and Lee suggested that nature's symmetry was flawed. For example, neutrinos always spin in a left-handed direction. In contrast, electrons can spin in both directions. The discovery of asymmetry won Yang and Lee the Nobel Prize for Physics just a year later. They also proposed a way to restore perfect left–right symmetry to nature: every right-handed particle might have a left-handed particle, and vice versa. This means that every particle must have a mirror partner; for example, the mirror neutrinos would be right-handed. Considered together, the real world and the mirror world would restore the symmetry that appears to be lacking in each.

Some scientists speculate that there might be a parallel universe containing mirror galaxies, mirror stars, mirror planets – even mirror life. If you did encounter your mirror-matter twin, you would pass right through him or her. You'd also be invisible to your twin.

Mirror matter doesn't interact with ordinary matter, making it difficult to find. We can't even see mirror matter. No mirror matter has yet been discovered or made in the laboratory. Some scientists believe that if this matter could be captured and placed near ordinary matter, it would absorb heat from its surroundings. This heat would radiate as 'mirror heat', which could be the source of limitless energy without violating the second law of thermodynamics (see p. 78).

Is there plenty of room at the bottom?

Richard Feynman (1918–88)

Nanotechnology is the engineering of machines at the molecular level.

In 1959, before he won the 1965 Nobel Prize for Physics, Feynman gave a visionary talk called 'There's Plenty of Room at the Bottom'. He proposed that 'the principles of physics … do not speak against the possibility of manoeuvring things atom by atom' or of building molecular-sized machines. The advance of nanotechnology – the technology that deals with objects smaller than 100 nanometres (a nanometre is millionth of a millimetre, about ten times the size of an individual atom) – has fulfilled his prophecy.

Another milestone in the short history of nanotechnology was the publication of *The Engines of Creation* (1986), a book by Eric Drexler, who is sometimes called the father of nanotechnology. In this futuristic book, Drexler envisions nanorobots or nanobots: hypothetical self-replicating intelligent machines too small to be seen by the naked eye. Like biological cells they'd be able to make copies of themselves. In theory, they could build anything as long as they had a ready supply of the right materials, a set of instructions and a source of energy.

Some scientists dismiss this idea as science fiction. To build nanobots, nanotechnologists must provide these machines with 'magic fingers'. Within the constraints of a space of one nanometre, manipulation of atoms isn't easy, because the fingers of a manipulator arm must themselves be made out of atoms. It appears that there isn't enough room to accommodate all the fingers necessary to have complete control of the process.

Damned if you do and damned if you don't

1961
USA

Joseph Heller (1923–99)

A situation in which a desired solution is impossible because of illogical rules.

In Heller's classic novel, *Catch-22* (1961), Yossarian, a bombardier serving in Italy during the Second World War, tries to escape from flying missions by getting himself declared insane. Doc Daneeka, the army surgeon, agrees that he has to ground anyone who's crazy, all one has to do is ask.

> 'And then you can ground him?' Yossarian asked.
> 'No. Then I can't ground him.'
> 'You mean there's a catch?'
> 'Sure there's a catch,' Doc Daneeka replied, 'Catch-22. Anyone who wants to get out of combat duty isn't really crazy.'

Catch-22 is an existential paradox, and the phrase is now widely used in everyday language, often incorrectly. Logic and mathematics thrive on paradoxes – the statements that sound reasonable but lead to self-contradictory conclusions.

Four paradoxes devised by the 5th-century-BC Greek philosopher Zeno are some of the oldest known paradoxes. The paradox of the arrow says that a flying arrow is at rest: at every instant of its flight the arrow occupies a space just its own size, meaning at every instant of its flight it is at rest. This paradox is based on the assumption that time is made up of discrete instants which are indivisible. Therefore, we can't have a speed at an instant (speed is distance travelled divided by elapsed time, but there's no elapsed time at an instant). The modern concept of instantaneous speed, which allows us to calculate how fast an object is travelling at a given instant, resolves the paradox.

See also RUSSELL'S PARADOX, p. 99.

Superchilled and spurious

N. N. Fedyakin

Scientists worried that if released from the lab, it would propagate itself by feeding on natural water, turning our planet into another freezing Venus.

We now know that polywater doesn't exist, but the 'discovery' fooled hundreds of scientists worldwide who churned out a stream of research papers from 1962 to 1974 describing its incredible properties. The story of polywater began when Fedyakin, a Russian scientist, claimed the discovery of a water-like liquid, which he called 'anomalous water' (American scientists named it 'polywater'). This gel-like substance was formed during condensation of water vapour in quartz capillary tubes. It was claimed that it had a density about 40 per cent higher than water; it boiled at about 540°C and froze at −40°C into a glassy substance quite unlike ice.

The bubble of scientific enthusiasm burst when carefully controlled analysis of minuscule samples provided by Fedyakin showed that it was contaminated badly by organic compounds. When polywater disappeared from the scientific world, it found a new home in *Star Trek*'s science fiction universe, where it belonged in the first place.

Why did polywater become a popular subject for research in spite of the fact that not many scientists had actually tested the substance? Most of the polywater frenzy was fuelled by the wide coverage of polywater stories by the media. When it became a popular subject, many scientists used the opportunity to attract the attention of the media and their peers at meetings. Even scientists like their fifteen minutes of fame. Score: Andy Warhol, 1; science, 0.

A very brave and prophetic book

Rachel Carson (1907–64)

Silent Spring **triggered the modern environmental movement.**

This 'prophetic book', remarked the Australian cartoonist, poet and philosopher Michael Leunig, 'popularised the scientific truth that humanity's degradation of the natural environment was causing dire imbalance in the ecological order – rivers were dying, species were disappearing and others growing in plague proportions as a consequence of humanity's chemical imperialism and reckless insensitivity and ignorance about nature'. This so-called chemical imperialism was the use of toxic pesticides encouraged by multinational chemical companies. These companies attacked Carson as a 'hysterical woman' unqualified to write such a book, while a *Time* magazine review in 1962 panned the book for 'oversimplifications and downright errors'. Nonetheless, in 1999 Carson was on *Time*'s list of the 100 most influential people of the 20th century for 'her very brave book', and in 2006 the *Atlantic* magazine ranked her 39th on its list of the 100 most influential Americans of all time.

Carson, a marine biologist and the author of an earlier highly successful book, *The Sea Around Us* (1951), was a thorough researcher and spent years painstakingly investigating the harmful effects of pesticides on wildlife and human health. The alarm she raised was so loud that it couldn't be ignored for long. Within a year a government panel accepted most of Carson's claims.

Silent Spring isn't a compendium of scientific facts, it's literature in its own right. 'It was a spring without voices. On the mornings that had once throbbed with the dawn chorus of scores of bird voices there was now no sound; only silence lay over the fields and woods and marsh.'

See also DDT IS A POTENT PESTICIDE, p. 138.

A new way of thinking about old problems

1962
USA

Thomas Kuhn (1922–96)

A paradigm shift is a fundamental change in underlying assumptions.

The term 'paradigm shift' was first used by Kuhn in his book *The Structure of Scientific Revolutions* (1962), one of the most popular academic books of the 20th century. As a graduate physics student, Kuhn read Aristotle and Newton's works and realised how different were their concepts of matter and motion. This and other similar observations in the history of science – where there was a fundamental change in paradigm or the framework of thought – led him to the idea that science doesn't develop by the orderly accumulation of facts and theories, but by the 'tradition-shattering complements to the tradition-bound activity of normal science'. He called these shifts in paradigms scientific revolution.

To Kuhn, normal science – 'research firmly based upon one or more past scientific achievements, achievements that some particular scientific community acknowledges for a time as supplying the foundation for its further practice' – is simply 'puzzle-solving'. Revolutionary science, on the other hand, involves a complete revision of existing scientific beliefs and practices. The development of science isn't uniform, but has alternating 'normal' and 'revolutionary' phases. The worlds before and after a paradigm shift are absolutely different.

Kuhn's book made the word 'paradigm' highly popular. Even the *New Yorker* magazine was inspired to publish a cartoon in which a woman exclaims: 'Dynamite, Mr. Gerston! You're the first person I ever heard use "paradigm" in real life.' In 2007 Google listed 42 million pages for 'paradigm', of which 2.6 million were 'paradigm shifts' (in real life, we hope).

Fast or fiction?

Various physicists

1962
USA

Tachyons are theoretical particles that travel faster than light.

> *There was a young girl named Miss Bright*
> *Who could travel much faster than light.*
> *She departed one day,*
> *In an Einsteinian way,*
> *And came back on the previous night.*

If Einstein had read this relativistic limerick, he would have said that Miss Bright had 'no possibility of existence', the phrase he used for speeds greater than the speed of light in his 1905 paper on special relativity (see p. 104). In 1962 a group of physicists went against Einstein's speed rule and proposed particles that could travel faster than light. They said that Einstein's rule didn't apply to these particles that were already moving faster than light. In 1967 the American physicist Gerard Feinberg named them tachyons (after Greek *tachus*, 'swift').

Weird tachyons, theoretically speaking, are always travelling faster than light – they're 'born' with speeds greater than light. When tachyons lose energy, they gain speed. When they gain energy, they slow down. Infinite energy is required to slow down a tachyon to the speed of light.

Most physicists have given up the idea that tachyons might be real. Nevertheless, they still keep on popping up in many new physics theories. For the time being Einstein's speed rule remains sacrosanct and tachyons don't exist. But it hasn't stopped them entering into the New Age world. Beware of enterprising New Agers who claim that they've harnessed the power of tachyons.

1965
USA

Measuring the universe's temperature

Arno Penzias (b. 1933)
and Robert Wilson (b. 1936)

The leftover warmth from the primeval fireball fills the universe today.

The universe began when an unimaginably dense and unimaginably hot speck of matter exploded spontaneously. The newly born universe was so hot that electrons and nuclei couldn't combine to form matter. The free-moving electrons scattered the photons, making the universe opaque. After 380,000 years the universe cooled to about 4,500°C and electrons and nuclei could combine to form the first hydrogen atoms. The universe now became transparent and photons were free to escape as gamma rays. As the universe continued cooling and expanding the wavelength of the radiation stretched. It changed from short wavelength gamma rays to longer wavelength X-rays, ultraviolet rays, visible light, and after 13.7 billion years into microwaves. This remnant radiation, usually referred to as the cosmic microwave background, can be detected anywhere. It has a temperature of −270°C (3°C above absolute zero).

In 1963 Bell Labs assigned radio astronomers Penzias and Wilson the task of tracing the radio noise that was interfering with the development of a communications satellite. Using a big, dish-shaped antenna, they detected a signal that seemed to come from the whole sky. When they inspected the antenna they found that pigeons were living in it. They cleaned the pigeon droppings, but the signal still remained. The signal was eventually identified as the cosmic microwave background radiation.

Penzias and Wilson's discovery, for which they were awarded the 1978 Nobel Prize for Physics, provided the most powerful proof for the big bang theory (see p. 125).

Not so fuzzy thinking

Lotfi Zadeh (b. 1921)

**Fuzzy logic provides a human-like way of dealing with
imprecise problems that have more than one solution.**

Fuzzy logic has its roots in the set theory. An object is either in a set
or not. There's no middle ground: either a number is odd, or it
isn't; either you belong to the set of beautiful people, or you don't.
This binary true–false, yes–no or 1–0 approach works well for computers, but fails miserably in the real world. In the ancient times
Pluto thought there was a third region beyond true and false, but
in our times Zadeh looked for shades of grey between true and false
when he asked: 'To what degree is something true or false?'

Let's consider a set of 'tall' people: everyone, say, over 175 centimetres is a member of this set. But what about someone who is
170 centimetres? The set theory refuses membership, but fuzzy
logic allows everyone some degree of membership because it measures membership not as 0 or 1, but as *between* 0 and 1. Fuzzy logic
has precise mathematical rules for vague expressions such as 'some-
what tall' or 'not really tall'.

Russian-born Zadeh was a professor of computer science at the
University of California, Berkeley, when he came up with the idea
that has now even made washing machines smart. How did he
come up with the word 'fuzzy'? He tried 'soft', 'unsharp', 'blurred'
and 'elastic', but in the end decided: 'I couldn't think of anything
more accurate so settled on "fuzzy".' Smart thinking!

The little green men who tuned out

Jocelyn Bell (Burnell) (b. 1943)

Pulsars (short for pulsating stars) are rotating neutron stars that release regular bursts of radio waves.

Bell, a Cambridge University research student, had the sole responsibility for operating a radio telescope and analysing the data. The telescope – an array of radio detectors spread over an area of more than four acres – was designed by her supervisor, the astronomer Antony Hewish, for the study of quasars (star-like objects that emit powerful radio waves). After the first few weeks, Bell noticed some unusual markings – she called them 'scruff' – on the charts spewed by the telescope. Bell at once realised that they were definitely not from quasars. Closer examination showed that they were a series of intense pulses. Initially, Bell and Hewish thought the signals were from some extraterrestrial intelligence and dubbed them LGM (little green men).

In fact, Bell had discovered the first evidence of a pulsar. When the news of the discovery broke out 'the press descended, and when they discovered a woman was involved they descended even faster', Bell recalls. 'I had my photograph taken standing on a bank [of detectors], sitting on a bank, standing on a bank examining bogus records: one of them even had me running down the bank waving my arms in the air – Look happy dear, you've just made a Discovery! (Archimedes doesn't know what he missed!)'

But this happy story has a rather unfortunate ending. Hewish was given a share of the 1974 Nobel Prize for Physics 'for his decisive role in the discovery of the pulsars', instead of Bell, who made the original observations.

See also RADIO ASTRONOMY, p. 135.

The modern-day Neptune that rules the Pacific

1969
USA

Jacob Bjerknes (1897–1975)

ENSO is a weather pattern that has major consequences for weather around the globe.

Every three to seven years, the central Pacific experiences a rise in surface temperature. When this huge mass of warm water moves eastwards to the normally colder waters off the coast of Peru, it produces a dramatic climate pattern. Long before its global impact became known, the Peruvian fisherman had given it the name El Niño (Spanish for 'the Christ child' because it usually happens around Christmas). In El Niño years, warm, moist air hangs around the middle of the Pacific bringing heavy rain in South America, but severe drought in the rainforests of Borneo to the farms of Australia.

In normal years, strong steady winds, called trade winds, blow from the east to the west across the Pacific. As the warm surface water moves to the west, the cold water from below replaces the warm surface water in the east. The warm waters in the west warm the air above creating a system of low pressure and turbulent tropical rainstorms. This large-scale redistribution of air mass between the eastern and western Pacific is known as the Southern Oscillation.

Norwegian-born Bjerknes, a meteorologist at the University of California, suggested that many long-term variations in the world's climate were due to large-scale interactions between the oceans and the atmosphere. He put the whole picture together when he linked El Niño and the Southern Oscillation. The combined phenomenon is called ENSO. It's possible that global warming could affect the frequency and strength of ENSO.

The particle zoo

1970s

Particle physicists around the world

The standard model of particle physics is a theory that explains matter and the forces of nature.

All elementary particles fit into two categories: fermions and bosons. Fermions are the particles of matter; they're only created in particle–antiparticle pairs. Bosons are particles that transmit force by the exchange of an intermediate particle peculiar to that force. The universe is held together by four types of fundamental forces: the strong force, the electromagnetic force, the weak force, and gravity. The strong force (which holds nuclei together) is mediated by gluons, the electromagnetic force (which is confined to particles that carry an electric charge) by photons, the weak force (which is involved in the formation of the chemical elements) by W and Z bosons, and gravity by hypothetical particles called gravitons. The standard model does not include gravity.

There are two classes of fermions: leptons and quarks. Both contain six particles: leptons – electron, electron neutrino, muon, muon neutrino, tau, tau neutrino; quarks – up quark, down quark, strange quark, charm quark, top quark, bottom quark. There are three generations of fermions. The first generation particles make up the ordinary matter. The second and third generation particles are produced in high-energy reactions and decay quickly into first-generation particles.

All this sounds very complex, but if we want to solve the mystery of the universe we must unravel the heart of the matter. The standard model has been validated by experiments, except for one particle called Higgs boson, which is still to be observed. We can expect to hear the shout of 'Eureka!' any day.

Floppy in the disk drive

Alan Shugart (b. 1930)

1970
USA

A floppy disk is a round platter of flexible Mylar plastic, coated with a thin layer of magnetic material, which can store computer data.

In early computers data was stored on punched cards in which each alphanumeric character was uniquely identified by holes punched in one or more rows of one of the 80 columns. This slow method was replaced by hard disk drives, as big as washing machines, which were introduced in 1955 by IBM. The next milestone came in 1970 when Shugart, an engineer at IBM, developed a disk drive that used a removable plastic disk only eight inches in diameter. The disk, which held a mere 200 kilobytes of data, was soon nicknamed 'floppy' because it was flexible. In 1976 Shugart developed the 5¼-inch floppy disk drive. When IBM introduced its PC in 1981 this floppy was the logical choice for a disk drive (see p. 177). The 3½-inch floppy was introduced by Sony in 1981.

Until recently the floppy disk provided the cheapest and the easiest way to store data or transfer data from one PC to another, but now they've been replaced by CD/DVD and flash memory drives. We'll keep this floppy story short, as if you read any more about computers you might start looking for the scroll bar to get to the next page!

1971
USA

The ubiquitous chips
Ted Hoff Jr (b. 1937)

The microprocessor, or microchip, started the electronic and computing revolution.

Called 4004, the first microprocessor was a silicon chip barely the size of a fingernail. But it packed in the computing power of ENIAC, the world's first working electronic digital computer built in 1946, which filled an entire room.

The story of 4004 started in 1969 when Hoff was working at Intel. A Japanese calculator company asked Intel to produce an integrated circuit, a computer chip, for its new programmable calculators. 'The calculators required a large number of chips, all of them quite expensive and it looked, quite frankly, as if it would tax all our design capability', he recalled later. Faced with this problem Hoff came up with an ingenious solution: why not place all the computing circuitry on one chip? The first programmable computer on a tiny silicon chip was born. Unlike the chips of the time, it wasn't hardwired for specific tasks. It worked with a set of instructions – software – to do its task.

It was christened 4004 because Hoff and his colleagues, Federico Faggin and Stanley Mazor, had planned to place 4004 transistors on the chip. The final chip had about 2,300 transistors (and for the technically minded, a clock speed of 108 kilohertz and 4-bit data bus). In 1979 Intel produced 8088 (29,000 transistors, 4.77 megahertz, 8-bit data bus). This had enough power to run IBM's first personal computer which was launched in 1981 (see p. 177). The rest is history (which can't be written now without the help of microchips).

The universe has to be the way it is

1973
Poland

Brandon Carter (b. 1942)

The universe has the right conditions for the existence of life.

There's nothing special about the conditions on this planet. There's no reason why things should be different anywhere else in the universe. In other words, one's location is unlikely to be special, or to put it bluntly, wherever or whenever we are, it's nothing special. This is known as the 'Copernicus principle' after Copernicus, who in 1543 said that Earth is not the centre of the universe.

In contrast, the anthropic principle (from Greek *anthropos*, 'human beings') maintains that the human beings hold a special place in the universe. The fundamental laws of physics that govern the universe are not the result of chance but somehow fine-tuned to allow the existence of intelligent life. If, for example, the force of gravity were slightly different than it is now, there would be no Sun-like stars anywhere.

The term 'anthropic principle' was proposed by Carter, a British cosmologist, in 1973 at a symposium in Poland commemorating Copernicus's 500th birthday. He suggested two versions of the principle: (1) the weak anthropic principle: the conditions in the universe are compatible with our existence; and (2) the strong anthropic principle: the universe must have those properties which would allow intelligent life within it at some stage. Other scientists have suggested different possible implications of the strong principle, including that the universe was 'designed' with the goal of sustaining human beings. This has been interpreted as evidence for a creator.

1973
USA

Brave new genetics

Stanley Cohen (b. 1935)
and Herbert Boyer (b. 1936)

Genetic engineering is the name given to a number of cutting-and-splicing techniques in which a gene is cut from one kind of organism and pasted into another.

The oldest genetic engineering technique is known as recombinant DNA technology. It was pioneered at Stanford University by two molecular geneticists, Cohen and Boyer. In this technique a DNA strand is cut with an enzyme. The fragment is then placed in a solution containing plasmids, small circular pieces of genetic material found in bacteria. The DNA fragment combines with a plasmid to form a new gene. The new gene, when placed in a solution containing normal bacterium, enters the bacterium. The bacterium then treats the new gene as its own and begins to produce the protein according to the new gene code. If, for example, the new code is for producing insulin, the bacterium will start producing insulin.

In fact, in 1982 human insulin, produced by bacteria that had received the appropriate human gene, became the first product of the genetic revolution to reach the medical marketplace. Another application of this revolution is gene therapy, in which a gene that's missing or defective is replaced with a correct one.

The rapid growth of genetic engineering is posing medical, philosophical, ethical, theological and social questions for which there are no easy answers. At what point do we cross the line from medical goals of preventing or treating diseases to non-medical purposes of enhancing desired traits? How far should we go?

A link to our past

Donald Johanson (b. 1943)

1974
Ethiopia

Lucy was the greatest fossil discovery of the 20th century.

Fossil and molecular studies show that humans evolved from primates who appeared about 55 million years ago (MYA), after the demise of the dinosaurs. The last common ancestor of humans, gorillas and chimpanzees lived between 8 and 6 MYA. About 6 MYA early 'proto-humans' called *Ardipithecus* split off from chimpanzees. These tree-friendly creatures shared traits with gorillas and chimpanzees.

American anthropologist Johanson was surveying for fossils near a river in Ethiopia when he discovered a 1.1-metre-tall fossil of a human ancestor who walked on Earth 3.2 MYA. Belonging to the species called *Australopithecus afarensis*, the fossil is 'the missing link' between apes and humans that anthropologists had long been searching for. Johanson decided to name the fossil Lucy when the popular Beatles' song 'Lucy in the Sky with Diamonds' was played at celebrations that night. Lucy may not be the direct link to humans because the human family tree has so many different branches. 'So, we can't be certain that she herself was actually on the direct line', says Johanson. 'We are certain that her bones are so different from early humans or human ancestors that she was a distinctive and different species.'

The fossil of a three-year-old *A. afarensis* was discovered in 2000 just four kilometres from the site where Lucy was found. The infant who lived about 3.3 MYA has been dubbed Lucy's baby. Lucy and her baby will help anthropologists understand the evolutionary sequence of changes that produced a walking hominid from a tree-dwelling ape.

Designer 'magic bullets'

1975
Switzerland
and UK

Niels Jerne (1911–94); Georges Köhler
(1946–95) and César Milstein (1927–2002)

**Monoclonal antibodies are pure protein molecules used
in diagnosing and treating many diseases.**

Antibodies, monoclonal or otherwise, are specialised protein molecules released by *B* cells, members of a class of white blood cells called lymphocytes. Antibodies are an important part of the immune system's response to invading organisms. The immune system has the ability to make millions of different antibodies, each able to 'recognise' a specific antigen.

A monoclonal antibody is a highly specific antibody, selected to recognise a particular antigen, but with the advantage that it can be mass-produced outside the body. By merging monoclonal antibody technology, genetic engineering researchers have taken nature's formidable antibody-synthesising system a step further. They can now produce novel antibody molecules that combine portions of one antibody-encoding gene with segments of another, yielding 'designer' antibodies for specific purposes.

Immunologists Jerne and Köhler of the Basel Institute for Immunology and Milstein of Cambridge University were awarded the 1984 Nobel Prize for Physiology or Medicine for their discovery of the principle for the production of monoclonal antibodies. Their work promised a revolution in diagnosing and treating cancer. Whether used as 'naked' antibodies or armed with radioactive isotopes or toxins, these 'magic bullets' – as monoclonal antibodies were soon rechristened by the popular press – could specifically seek out and destroy cancer cells without harming normal cells. However, the much-touted monoclonal antibody has earned the reputation of being a 'microscopic emperor without clothes'. Although trials with animals have shown many successes, problems have arisen in similar trails with humans.

Mountains are not cones

Benoit Mandelbrot (b. 1924)

1975
USA

Fractals are geometric patterns that show self-similarity, that is, they look essentially the same as you zoom in and zoom out.

Most patterns in nature aren't formed of simple geometric figures such as squares, triangles and circles, but of shapes that are jagged and broken up. Before Mandelbrot, mathematicians disdained describing such shapes mathematically. Classical geometry cannot describe the shape of a cloud, a mountain, a coastline or a tree. 'Clouds are not spheres', as Mandelbrot says, 'mountains are not cones, and bark is not smooth, nor does lightning travel in a straight line'.

Born in Poland, Mandelbrot moved to the United States in 1958. In 1975 he invented a new geometry of irregular and fragmented patterns around us. He called these beautifully complex patterns fractals (from the Latin *fract*, 'broken'). 'Small parts are the same as the big parts; that's the definition of fractal', says Mandelbrot. 'A cloud is made of billows upon billows that look like clouds. As you come closer to a cloud you don't get something smooth but irregularities at a smaller scale.' Ferns, cauliflowers, snowflakes, rivers, mountains and lightning – they all are fractals. Fractals can be described by simple mathematical equations that can be used to generate computer images.

Fractal geometry is now used to compress computer images; locate underground oil deposits; build dams; understand corrosion, acid rain, earthquakes and hurricanes; study global climate change; and even to model booms and busts of stock markets. All this and more thanks to a mathematician who said: 'The beauty of geometry is that it is a language of extraordinary subtlety.'

1978
England

Babies like any other

Patrick Steptoe (1913–88)
and Robert Edwards (b. 1925)

**IVF involves mixing eggs and sperm in a laboratory dish
and then implanting the resulting embryos into the womb.**

As an obstetrician and gynaecologist Steptoe was often faced with the extreme sadness of women who were unable to conceive. In most cases the cause of infertility was blocked fallopian tubes, which prevented the fertilisation and movement of an embryo to uterus for development. He met Edwards, a professor of reproductive biology at Cambridge University, at a scientific meeting in 1968 in London. Edwards had developed a way to fertilise human eggs in a laboratory.

They decided to team up and spent years perfecting an IVF technique. Steptoe used a fibre-optic device called a laparoscope to siphon eggs directly from infertile women. Once fertilised in vitro (outside the body) they could be transferred into the uterus. After dozens of failed attempts, success came in 1978 when Lesley Brown gave birth by caesarean section to the first 'test tube' baby.

The astonishing feat made Steptoe and Edwards instant celebrities. Many religious groups were horrified by the event and they accused the doctors of playing god. A British magazine ran a cover story claiming that the test tube babies were 'the biggest threat since the atom bomb'. IVF is now considered a routine procedure. More than 3 million women worldwide have used IVF successfully since the birth of a bouncing baby of 5 lb 12 oz. Aptly named Louise Joy Brown, this baby has now grown up into a healthy young woman.

Computers by the zillions

A team of IBM engineers

1981
USA

The introduction of the IBM PC revolutionised offices, schools and homes.

I think there is a world market for about five computers.
   – Thomas Watson, Chairman, IBM, 1943
There is no reason for anyone to have a computer in their home.
   – Ken Olson, President, Digital Equipment, 1977
640K [of memory] ought to be enough for everyone.
   – Bill Gates, CEO, Microsoft, 1981

Within months of its launch on 12 August 1981, the IBM PC proved them all wrong. By today's standards it was a Mickey Mouse: 8-bit Intel 8088 microprocessor running at 4.77 megahertz, 64 kilobytes of random access memory (RAM), single-sided 5¼-inch floppy disk drive capable of storing 160 kilobytes, and a black-and-white monitor (colour monitor was optional). It didn't have a hard drive; application programs had to be loaded into the computer's RAM.

In fact, the IBM PC was not the first PC. That milestone in the history of computers goes to the Altair 8800 with an early Intel processor and 1 kilobyte of RAM. Launched in 1977, it was sold in kit form. However, IBM popularised the term 'personal computer' and its acronym PC, which is now used for all desktop or portable computers.

The IBM PC's operating system, called Microsoft disk operating system (MS-DOS), was designed by Microsoft Corporation, a company formed by Bill Gates in 1977. The instant popularity of the PC stimulated two industries: a software industry for developing applications, and a completely new industry of computer magazines including reviews of new hardware and software, and tips and hints for using them.

Something to brighten your day

1982
USA

Arthur A. Stone (b. 1951)

No more blue Mondays.

You may still believe in blue Mondays, but in 1982 Stone, a psychologist at Stony Brook University in New York, relegated this belief to folklore. He said that no matter what people claim, Monday moods turn out to be no worse than those on other workdays. His studies of mood, stress and physical illness on middle-class white-collar workers showed that positive moods were higher on Fridays, Saturdays and Sundays. Moods worsened on Mondays and stayed about the same up to, and including, Thursdays.

So, why is Monday viewed as grim and unpleasant? Maybe it's just the contrast with Sunday – the idyllic day – that produces perception that Monday is the worst day of the week. Or maybe people adhere to a blue Monday cultural myth, which causes them to choose Monday when asked for the worst day of the week. Other recent psychological studies also suggest that blue Monday is primarily a result of the expectations imposed by the myth.

Researchers have supposedly turned Monday into a lighter shade of blue, but for some of us – no matter what they or the blues guitarist 'T-Bone' Walker say – Monday remains a darker shade of blue.

> They call it stormy Monday
> But Tuesday's just as bad
> Wednesday's worse
> And Thursday's also sad.

When a computer catches cold

Fred Cohen (b. 1956)

Cohen coined the term 'computer virus' to describe a program that can 'infect' other programs. It can insert copies of itself into another program, which may also act as a virus, and so the infection spreads.

The idea came to Cohen while he was working on his PhD thesis at the University of Southern California. 'All at once, a light bulb came on, and I said, "Aha!"', Cohen recalls. 'Within a few seconds I knew how to write the program and that it would work.' He wrote the program and added it to a minicomputer's program. The virus seized control of the computer within a few minutes. In a paper published the next year he prophetically wrote that viruses could 'spread through computer networks in the same way as they spread through computers' and could 'wreak havoc on modern government, financial, business, and academic institutions'.

The first virus for personal computers was created in 1986 by two hackers (programmers who intentionally design viruses) in Pakistan. Called 'The Brain', it piggy-backed on a program held on floppy disks. Viruses on floppy disks were a nuisance, but they could infect a computer only when the disks were passed around. Now most viruses travel via email with alarming speed. They usually replicate themselves by automatically mailing themselves to addresses in the victim's email address book.

Viruses can be detected and destroyed by antivirus programs, but most computer experts believe that it's mathematically impossible to write a generic program that will detect all present and future programs.

A gut feeling

1984
Australia

Robin Warren (b. 1937)
and Barry Marshall (b. 1951)

Life-threatening stomach ulcers are caused by bacteria.

In 1979 when Warren, a pathologist, was examining tissues taken from the stomach lining of a patient suffering from a stomach ulcer, he noticed a tiny blue line on the surface. He looked through a higher power lens of his microscope, and was surprised to see that it looked like bacteria. When he stained them, there were millions of them. 'These things were well and truly alive and growing in vast numbers', he recalls. The conventional wisdom at the time was that stomach ulcers were caused by weak stomach linings or high acid levels, not by bacterial infections.

In 1981 Marshall, a young gastroenterologist, joined Warren and both continued research on the corkscrew-like bacteria, *Helicobacter pylori*. A year later when they announced their hypothesis, it was ridiculed by critics who said that bacteria can't survive in the high acidic environment of the stomach. In 1984 the prestigious medical journal *Lancet* published the details of their discovery. But the conservative medical profession still refused to believe them. To prove critics wrong, Marshall swallowed a small dose of the live bacteria. He duly developed a stomach ulcer, which was promptly healed with antibiotics. In spite of this amazing act of self-experimentation, it took another ten years before antibiotics became the standard treatment for stomach ulcers.

Warren and Marshall were awarded the 2005 Nobel Prize for Physiology or Medicine for proving that the stomach ulcer isn't a painful chronic condition but an infectious disease that can be cured easily.

Bar coding humans

Alec Jeffreys (b. 1950)

1984
UK

A technique that provides a visual pattern of a part of a DNA that's unique to each individual.

Jeffreys, a geneticist at the University of Leicester, was studying a gene from a lump of grey seal meat when, purely by chance, he found a bit of DNA inside the gene, 'which was the key to unlock the door on genetic fingerprinting'. He recalls: 'So for me it was very much a Eureka moment, my life literally changed in five minutes flat, in a darkroom when I pulled out that first DNA finger-print and saw just what we'd stumbled upon.'

The DNA helix is made up of four building blocks, called base pairs A, C, T and G, which can be linked in only four combinations: A–T, C–G, T–A, G–C. The sequence of these four base pairs along the length of the strand makes one DNA different from another. The technique of DNA fingerprinting is a complex one, but the end result is an X-ray film with light and dark patterns, very much like a bar code. This 'bar code' is unique to each individual, except for identical twins. Estimates of the chance of two individuals matching vary from one in a billion to one in a trillion.

DNA fingerprinting is now commonly used for identification: establishing family relationships in paternity or maternity disputes; analysing patterns of migration or proving claims of ethnicity; or identifying crime suspects from DNA (from samples such as blood, saliva or hair) gathered at crime scenes. It can also be used to identify smuggled or poached animals.

The hole in the sky

A team of scientists from the British Antarctic Survey

The ozone hole is the dramatic loss of the ozone layer over Antarctica.

The ozone layer is a band of ozone gas in the stratosphere, an upper layer of the atmosphere. It absorbs harmful ultraviolet light and shields Earth from the worst of the Sun's radiation.

British scientists began studying the ozone layer in 1924, when Gordon Dobson of Oxford University designed and built an instrument to measure ozone levels in the ozone layer. They noticed only seasonal variations in the levels until the late 1970s. Thereafter it became clear that the ozone layer over Antarctica was fast depleting. They announced in 1985 that they'd found a puzzling gap or 'hole' – an area larger than Australia in size – in which the ozone layer had depleted by about 50 per cent. The hole now appears each year during the southern hemisphere spring. In 2006 it reached record proportions of more than three times the size of Australia. The hole is caused by chlorine released by chlorofluorocarbons (CFCs), synthetic chemicals used mainly in the northern hemisphere as refrigerants and as foaming agents for polymers. The use of CFCs has dropped, but we won't see the effects of the drop until about 2024.

The hole poses a risk to people living under it. Without any suitable protection, the increased ultraviolet light can cause rapid sunburn, skin cancer and eye problems such as cataracts. So, when you're in the southern hemisphere, the motto is: slip (on a shirt), slop (on suncream) and slap (on a hat).

Great 'soccer balls' of carbon

1985
USA

Robert Curl (USA, b. 1933); Harold Kroto (UK, b. 1939) and Richard Smalley (USA, b. 1943)

Like graphite and diamond, buckyballs – tiny, hollow molecules shaped like soccer balls – are a form of pure carbon.

The story of buckyballs began in 1984 when scientists discovered that when graphite is vaporised with laser it changes into a range of carbon molecules, which always contains an even number of atoms. Kroto became so intrigued by this result that he convinced Curl and Smalley to try graphite in the new laser vaporisation equipment they were using to study silicone chemistry. He was hoping to make long carbon chains, perhaps up to 33 atoms long. Smalley was sceptical that the experiment would prove anything novel. 'It seemed like a stupid idea at the time', he said later. That 'stupid idea' won Curl, Kroto and Smalley the 1996 Nobel Prize for chemistry.

The experiment did produce long carbon chains, but the trio were intrigued to find not only that carbon atoms tend to form molecules with an even number of atoms; but that the predominant clusters were 60-carbon groups. What, they wondered, was special about 60-carbon groups? How was each group forming a stable structure from 60 atoms? Kroto suggested that the 60-carbon molecule might resemble the American architect Buckminster Fuller's geodesic domes made from glass and metal. Smalley soon found that a perfect sphere with 60 vertices could be formed by interlocking twenty hexagons and twelve pentagons. They named this new form of carbon molecule 'buckminsterfullerness' in honour of Fuller, and it's become affectionately known as a 'buckyball'.

Scientists believe there are numerous uses for buckyballs: as a lubricant, as a semiconductor and as a catalyst. They have also synthesised tubelike buckyballs, which are, naturally, called 'buckytubes'.

Debunking a myth

1988
Italy

An international team of scientists

It has been venerated for centuries as the cloth used to wrap the body of Jesus Christ after crucifixion.

The shroud, a 4.3-metre long piece of linen, carries what appears to be the bloody imprint of a naked man lying with his hands crossed on his stomach. The image looks like a scorch and appears on only one side of the linen; it hasn't permeated the fibres. When first photographed in 1898 by Secondo Pia, an Italian lawyer and amateur photographer, the image resembled a photographic negative.

Because it first came to attention in 1357, the shroud has frequently been branded a 14th-century European forgery. In 1988 the Vatican agreed to a radiocarbon dating (see p. 144) of the relic. An international team of scientists analysed a sample, about the size of a postage stamp, and concluded that it was created between 1260 and 1390. This led to the Archbishop of Turin, the custodian of the shroud, admitting that the shroud was a hoax.

But some myths are not easy to debunk. Many so-called shroud scholars have claimed that the sample used in the 1988 tests was cut from a medieval patch woven into the shroud to repair fire damage. The shroud was indeed damaged in a church blaze in 1532 and was restored by nuns by patching holes with a new material. In 2005 Raymond Rogers, a retired American chemist, claimed that a microchemical test performed on a piece of shroud the size of a grain showed that the shroud was between 1,300 and 3,000 years old.

Too hot to handle

Stanley Pons (b. 1943) and
Martin Fleischmann (b. 1927)

1989
USA

Nuclear fusion takes place at very high temperature, but can it happen at room temperature?

When the nuclei of light elements join to form a new, heavier nucleus, the reaction releases tremendous amounts of energy. Starting a nuclear fusion requires a temperature greater than the Sun's. Scientists have yet to build a successful fusion reactor. If a way can be found to start fusion at room temperature, it will be a potential source of limitless energy and will solve the world's energy problems.

On 23 March 1989 Stanley Pons and Martin Fleischmann, chemists at the University of Utah, astounded the world when they announced at a press conference that they'd discovered a way to produce nuclear fusion in a glass jar at room temperature. Their bench-top fusion reactor consisted of two electrodes – one palladium, the other platinum – immersed in a glass jar of heavy water (water containing deuterium in place of ordinary hydrogen). This simple apparatus was claimed to produce heat energy ten times more than the electrical energy passed through the electrodes. The chemists also claimed that the reaction generated gamma radiation. When hundreds of scientists around the world tried to replicate the experiment, the only thing they could find in their glass jars was cold water.

Most scientists don't consider cold fusion to be a real phenomenon. *New Scientist* magazine remarked in 1991 that the cold fusion saga 'has proved to be a stern reminder that scientists are just as vulnerable to the human failings of greed, vanity and spite as anyone else'.

1990
World

Tackling the genetic puzzle
Scientists around the globe

The Human Genome Project was one of the most ambitious scientific endeavours ever undertaken.

The human genome is the entire DNA, which consists of about 30,000 genes and about 3 billion base pairs (see p. 153). The DNA is arranged in 24 pairs of chromosomes, physically separate molecules that range in length from about 50 million to 250 million base pairs. Each chromosome contains many genes, the basic units of heredity. Each of the 100 trillion cells in the human body carries in its nucleus 23 pairs of chromosomes (46 in all), except sperm and egg which contain only a single copy of each chromosome (23 in each). A special pair of chromosomes determines the sex of a human. Cells of women have two X chromosomes, whereas those of men have one X and one Y chromosome.

Scientists have now mapped all chromosomes. The information, which would fill 200 500-page telephone directories, is helping scientists to find genes associated with dozens of genetic conditions and to develop thousands of new drugs for previously untreatable diseases.

In 1984 Robert Sinsheimer, then chancellor of the University of California at Santa Cruz, proposed that all human genes be mapped. Mapping started in 1988, though the project was launched officially in Europe and the USA in 1989 and 1990. It was completed in 2003. It will be years, maybe decades, before scientists completely unlock the mysteries hidden in the gene maps the Human Genome Project, the crown jewel of 20th-century biology, has helped create.

The brilliant web he wove

Tim Berners-Lee (b. 1955)

1991
Switzerland

WWW is the mass medium of this century.

In 1999, when British-born Berners-Lee made the list of *Time* magazine's 100 greatest minds of the 20th century, the magazine asked its readers to launch a search engine and type in the word 'enquire' ('British spelling, please', the magazine insisted). 'You'll get about 30,000 hits', the magazine exclaimed. 'It turns out you can "enquire" about nearly anything online these days.' The same exercise will now score millions of hits (14 million in 2007). Today, you can really enquire about anything online, as we all in one way or the other are entangled in the web Berners-Lee wove less than two decades ago.

It all began in 1989 when Berners-Lee was working at CERN, the European Laboratory for Particle Physics in Geneva. He proposed a hypertext project, the now familiar point-and-click system of navigating through information, to link CERN's personal computers with the internet. The following year, he designed a set of rules (HTTP or Hypertext Transfer Protocol) to link files together on computers across the internet, and a system of addresses (URLs or Uniform Resource Locators) to locate these files. He then designed the first browser to allow his creation to be seen – which he called World Wide Web after rejecting names such as the Mine of Information and Information Mesh – on any computer linked to the internet.

The first web page (http://info.cern.ch/hypertext/WWW/The-Project.html) was launched on 6 August 1991. It had no graphics, no dynamic images, just plain text. The rest is wow!

Ida's Dactyl

1993
USA

NASA's Galileo spacecraft

Dactyl is the first moon of an asteroid ever discovered.

Imagine playing cricket on Asteroid 243 Ida (each asteroid is assigned a catalogue number in chronological order of its discovery). Hit the ball hard and it would circle over your head and strike the surface behind you. Hit the ball gently and it would land in front of you. Drop it at eye level and it would take about 30 seconds to hit the ground. The cause of this weird behaviour is a combination of Ida's low and irregular gravity, rapid rotation and peanut-like shape (dimensions: 56 x 24 x 21 kilometres). Most asteroids have such idiosyncratic dynamics. Many of them also have tiny moons. Ida has Dactyl – the first known asteroid satellite, a mere 1.4 kilometres in diameter.

Dactyl was discovered by the Galileo spacecraft, launched in 1989 from the space shuttle Atlantis, which passed through the asteroid belt on its way to Jupiter. Astronomers found Ida's satellite on images sent by Galileo on 28 August 1993. Images were taken from a distance of about 3,900 kilometres. The discovery was confirmed a year later by the International Astronomical Union, which named the satellite Dactyl (derived from the Dactyli, a group of beings in Greek mythology who lived on Mount Ida).

The egg-shaped Dactyl orbits about 108 kilometres from Ida. It's most important geological features are more than a dozen craters larger than 80 kilometres in diameter. Some astronomers speculate that Ida and Dactyl were formed as a pair a billion or more years ago, when Ida's parent body was disrupted.

See also ASTEROIDS, p. 58.

Strange new worlds

Michel Mayor (b. 1942)
and Didier Queloz (b. 1966)

1995
France

The discovery of extra-solar planets – planets beyond the solar system – challenges the notion that our solar system is unique.

The idea of planets orbiting other stars has fascinated scientists since 1755 when the German philosopher Immanuel Kant proposed a theory for the formation of the solar system: a spinning cloud of gas and dust broke into rings that condensed to form the Sun and the planets. The search for extra-solar planets started in earnest in 1981 when Canadian astronomers observed dozens of Sun-like stars. Their decade-long search yielded nothing, but it encouraged other astronomers to continue looking for new worlds.

Michel Mayor and Didier Queloz of the University of Geneva shouted 'Eureka!' on 6 October 1995 when they announced the discovery of the first extra-solar planet. Working at Observatoire de Haute Provence in south-east France, they had discovered a planet orbiting a Sun-like star only 44 light years from the Sun. The planet – named 51 Pegasi b – orbits the star 51 Pegasi in the northern constellation Pegasus (the Winged Horse). It's a Jupiter-like gas-giant 140 times the mass of Earth, and so close to its star that it whips around it in a mere four days.

It seems that the Winged Horse has kicked open the gates of heavens for astronomers. They have since discovered more than 200 extra-solar planets; many of them are multi-planet systems. Most of them are gas giants, but scientists are enthusiastic about discovering Earth-like planets. Such planets probably lie within the habitable zones of the galaxy, zones where life on a planet is possible.

2004
UK

'I now have an answer to it'

Stephen Hawking (b. 1942)

What happens to information in matter destroyed by a black hole?

Sometimes the crushing weight of a dying star squeezes it into a point with infinite density. At this point, known as singularity, both space and time stop. The singularity is surrounded by an imaginary surface known as the event horizon, a kind of one-way spherical boundary. Nothing – not even light – can escape the event horizon. Such regions of space-time are called black holes.

In 1974 Hawking, a physicist best known for his popular science book, *A Brief History of Time* (1988), suggested that black holes are not that black after all. Once a black hole is formed it radiates energy and starts losing mass and will evaporate eventually. This radiation, known as Hawking radiation, is random. This means in a practical sense it carries no information and, therefore, all information about the matter that fell into a black hole is lost. But this violates the laws of physics and creates a problem known as the information paradox.

In 2004 Hawking reversed his belief and said: 'I have been thinking about this problem for 30 years, but I now have an answer to it … The black hole appears to form but later opens up and releases information about what fell in, so we can be sure of the past and we can predict the future.' It's comforting to know that the extreme gravitational fields of black holes do not make them anarchic and they still follow the good ol' laws of nature, at least according to Professor Hawking of Cambridge University.

From pizzas to nachos

International Astronomical Union (IAU)

2006
Czechoslovakia

The 'new' solar system – with only eight planets – reflects advances in our understanding of the heavenly bodies the ancient Greeks called *planetes*, or wanderers.

My Very Educated Mother Just Served Us Nine Pizzas – the mnemonic you learned at school to list the order of the nine planets (outwards from the Sun) is now without your favourite pizza for Pluto. After demoting Pluto, the IAU recommends that your mother should serve nachos instead: My Very Educated Mother Just Served Us Nachos. At its general assembly in Prague the IAU defined a 'planet' as a celestial body that: (a) is in orbit around the Sun; (b) is massive enough to have its self-gravity to pull itself into a round (or nearly round) shape; and (c) there are no other bodies in its path that it must sweep up as it goes around the Sun. Pluto fails to meet criterion (c). For in about twenty years, Pluto's 248-year orbit will bring it closer to the Sun than Neptune.

The IAU has created a new category of objects, called 'dwarf planets', for Pluto-like objects. This category includes Ceres, an asteroid discovered in 1801 (see p. 58), and Eris (formerly known as Xena), discovered in 2005. Pluto and Eris both reside in Kuiper belt, a belt of primordial icy bodies that surrounds the eight planets. More Kuiper-belt objects will be classified 'dwarf planets' in the coming years.

The IAU has also introduced a new term 'small solar system body' for all objects that orbit the Sun but are too small to be called a planet or a dwarf planet.

Removing the question mark

Intergovernmental Panel on Climate Change

The science is now clear; we can no longer ignore the evidence that human activities have caused global warming.

The Eiffel Tower's 20,000 sparkling bulbs went dark for five minutes on the eve of the launch of the report of the Intergovernmental Panel on Climate Change in Paris. This symbolic gesture acknowledged the unequivocal warning of the report that global warming is here and worsening. Achim Steiner – executive director of the United Nations Environmental Programme, which administers the panel along with the World Meteorological Organization – remarked that 2 February 2007 will be remembered as the day that the question mark was removed from the debate on whether human activities are causing climate change.

The major findings of the report – the work of 2,500 scientists from 113 countries – are:

- The atmospheric concentration of carbon dioxide – the main greenhouse gas – has risen from about 280 parts per million from pre-industrial levels to 379 parts per million in 2005.
- The eleven years from 1995 to 2005 have ranked among the twelve warmest years since records began in 1850.
- Mountain glaciers and snow cover have declined on average in both hemispheres.
- Our planet will warm between 1.1°C and 6.4°C this century.
- Sea level rises will range from 18 to 59 centimetres by 2100.
- There is at least a 90 per cent probability that extremes such as heatwaves and heavy rain will become more frequent, and tropical cyclones will become more intense.

See also GLOBAL WARMING, p. 93.

Index

The entries in bold are the main topics of stories.